World's GREATEST *Movie Trivia*

Pixar Edition

Catherine Olen

World's Greatest Movie Trivia
Pixar Edition

© 2021 Catherine Olen

First paperback edition April 2021
ISBN 978-1-64822-016-6 (paperback)
ISBN 978-1-64822-017-3 (eBook)

Published by Mouse Hangover
www.Mousehangover.com

Please note: Every effort has been made to ensure the accuracy of the information throughout this book. The information is believed to be accurate at the time of printing. The publisher and author are not responsible for errors or omissions, changes to details, or the consequences of the reader's reliance on the information provided.

Readers are welcome to contact the publisher for comments, updates, or questions.

Disclaimer

About the Author

 Catherine Olen has been visiting Disney parks since she was a small child and watching Disney films throughout her life. Olen fell in love with the films built through Walt Disney's imagination and has watched every film release ever since.

Olen first traveled to Walt Disney World at the age of thirty, immediately falling in love with the Florida parks. She has traveled to the Walt Disney World theme parks each year since and now travels to Orlando several times a year to revel in the new attractions and the classic favorites.

Olen now shares her love of all things Pixar in *World's Greatest Movie Trivia: Pixar Edition*.

Come Check Us Out

Check out new books, video, and news at
www.Mousehangover.com
Subscribe to Mouse Hangover
Parler - @CatherineOlen
MeWe - @CatherineOlen
Facebook - @WGMTPixarEdition
@WDWScavengerHunt

Rumble - @CatherineOlen

Telegram - @CatherineOlen

Gab - @CatherineOlen

Other books:

The Great Disneyland Scavenger Hunt
The Great Universal Studios Hollywood Scavenger Hunt
The Great Universal Orlando Scavenger Hunt
The Great Universal Studios Hollywood Scavenger Hunt
One Hundred Things to do at Disneyland Before you Die
One Hundred Things to do at Walt Disney World Before
     you Die
One Hundred Things to do at Universal Orlando Before
     you Die
One Hundred Things to do at Universal Studios
     Hollywood Before you Die
World's Greatest Movie Trivia: Disney Princess Edition

Dedication

To everyone who gave me their support and assistance in the process of finishing this book

To Every person that has fallen in love with Pixar films throughout the years

Lastly, my thanks to Walt Disney for the vision that created these amazing movies

Table of Contents

Introduction

My excitement with the Pixar films began in November 1995 when I arrived at the movie theater to see Disney's latest animated film. Toy Story would begin a new era in animated film with the first fully computer-generated production ever created. I was mesmerized by the new animation techniques with realistic detail never seen before. Along with everyone else in the theater, I realized that we were seeing history being made right before our eyes.

With each new film, I found new characters to pull at my heart. I sometimes cursed the story writers and animators who could make me cry over an adorable cowgirl doll left by the side of the road in a donation box or a monster who loved a child so much his heart broke when he had to leave her.

Over the years, the technology became so advance that I could swear that I was looking at the world beneath the ocean surface or a community aboard an enormous space vessel. The ability of the animators to make inanimate objects come to life seems to be boundless.

Now, over twenty-five years later, Pixar is still dazzling us with new stories and characters. I would like to dedicate this book to every person involved in the creative process that has gifted us these amazing films.

Toy Story

1. As you get the first glimpse of Andy's room, what store is colored on the first cardboard box you see?
    - a. Bank
    - b. Hotel
    - c. Saloon
    - d. Jail

2. What reward is offered on Mr. Potato Head according to the wanted poster?
    - a. Thirty Bzillion
    - b. Forty Bzillion
    - c. Fifty Quintillion
    - d. Fifty Bzillion

3. What color is the gun Mr. Potato Head has taped to his hand?
    - a. Orange
    - b. Blue
    - c. Green
    - d. Purple

4. Which of these is *not* one of the toys Mr. Potato Head holds up during playtime?
    - a. Rex
    - b. Bo Peep
    - c. Troll doll
    - d. Little People

5. Where is the safe Mr. Potato Head holds up located?
   a. Sack of coins
   b. Piggy Bank
   c. Under Andy's bed
   d. Inside the Bank box

6. What are the first words we hear from Woody when Andy pulls his drawstring?
   a. Somebody's poisoned the waterhole
   b. There a snake in my boot
   c. This town ain't big enough for the both of us
   d. Reach for the sky

7. When One-Eyed Bart shows his attack dog, what is his special power?
   a. Super stretch body
   b. Super bark
   c. Built-in force field
   d. Super speed

8. Where is the jail that Andy puts Mr. Potato Head in?
   a. The crib
   b. The jail box
   c. The toy box
   d. The closet

9. What does Andy use as a lasso to wrangle the cattle?
   a. Ball of yarn
   b. Robe sash
   c. Jump rope
   d. Hose

10. After Andy launches Woody off of the recliner and Woody lands on the chair, what does Andy yell out in triumph?
    a. Score
    b. Direct hit
    c. Victory
    d. Yeah

11. As Andy picks up Woody from the chair, what words are written on the pillow resting on the chair?
    a. Welcome
    b. Home Sweet Home
    c. Home is Where the Heart is
    d. Loving Family

12. When Andy lowers the side of the crib to pick up his sister, what is painted on the arch of the side of the crib?
    a. A pacifier
    b. A baby
    c. Rattles
    d. A baby bottle

13. What is Mr. Potato Head's nickname for Molly?
    a. Princess Drool
    b. Princess Fussy Pants
    c. Princess Molly
    d. Princess Ankle Biter

14. What is written on the side of the firetruck the little firemen get into?
    a. Tonka
    b. Preschool
    c. Little Tikes
    d. Playmobil

15. When Mr. Potato Head puts himself back together, what famous artist does he say he is?
    a. Van Gogh
    c. Pollock
    b. Monet
    d. Picasso

16. As Woody is getting ready for the staff meeting, which toy does he say "Draw" to?
    a. Speak and Spell
    a. Doodle pad
    a. Etch a Sketch
    a. Spirograph

17. When the nesting eggs separate themselves, how many eggs do you see?
    a. Six
    c. Five
    b. Four
    d. Three

> *Did you know?*
>
> As woody begins the staff meeting, the books on the shelf behind him are Pixar short cartoons' titles. Tin Toy and Knickknack are two of the first Pixar shorts created.

18. What does Woody use as a desk during the staff meeting?
    a. Tinker toy box
    c. Wooden Alphabet
    b. Board Game Box
    Blocks
    d. Books

19. How many pieces are in the Tinker toy® container according to the box?
    a. Forty-five
    c. Fifty-five
    b. Thirty-five
    d. Twenty-five

20. Which night of the week was the plastic toy corrosion awareness meeting?
    a. Monday
    c. Friday
    b. Thursday
    d. Tuesday

21. According to Mr. Potato Head, how long has Woody been Andy's favorite toy?
    a. Since first grade
    c. Since forever
    b. Since birth
    d. Since kindergarten

22. What is the name the plastic soldiers give to the operation to spy on the birthday party?
    a. Recon Plan Charlie
    c. Recon Plan Omega
    b. Recon Plan Alpha
    d. Recon Plan Foxtrot

23. Andy's mom tells the kids she has two kinds of chips, Cool Ranch and what other flavor?
    a. Barbeque
    c. Salt and vinegar
    b. Regular
    d. Cheese

24. What is the plastic soldier holding that Andy's mom stepped on?
    a. Grenade
    c. Metal detector
    b. Rifle
    d. Parachute

25. What is written on the plant tag the plastic soldiers hide in?
    - a. Desert Cactus
    - b. Radial Fichus
    - c. Forest Fantasy
    - d. Geranium

26. Which is *not* one of the gifts Andy opens on his birthday?
    - a. Bedsheets
    - b. Cowboy costume
    - c. Battle Ship™
    - d. Lunch box

27. What does the sergeant call Woody when Andy's mom pulls the surprise present out of the closet?
    - a. Mother bird
    - b. Poppa Smurf
    - c. High chief
    - d. Alpha one

28. What is written on the batteries that fall out of the baby monitor?
    - a. Cell Charger
    - b. Dura Life
    - c. Econo Charge
    - d. Power Cell

29. What does Andy's mom call to the boys when the kids are playing in Andy's room?
    - a. Time for cake
    - b. Time for games
    - c. Time to go
    - d. Time lunch

30. What sector does Buzz Lightyear say he was headed to when he gets to Andy's room?
    - a. Ten
    - b. Thirteen
    - c. Fourteen
    - d. Twelve

31. Which unit of the Space Rangers does Buzz Lightyear belong to?
    a. Universe patrol squad
    b. Alien protection unit
    c. Universe protection unit
    d. Planet protection unit

32. Which part of Buzz Lightyear's ship does he say he needs to repair?
    a. Structure system
    b. Guidance system
    c. Propulsion system
    d. Turbo boosters

33. Which toy is the first to shake hands with Buzz Lightyear when he introduces himself?
    a. Rex
    b. Slinky Dog
    c. Bo Peep
    d. Mr. Potato Head

34. As Woody chats with Bo Peep about the new toy, she says he has more gadgets on him than what?
    a. Inspector Gadget
    b. Supercomputer
    c. Kitchen drawer
    d. A Swiss Army Knife

35. What part of Buzz Lightyear is Hamm impressed with?
    a. His voice button
    b. His lasers
    c. His wingspan
    d. His height

36. Which character does John Ratzenberger voice in
    Toy Story?
    a. Rex   c. Slinky Dog
    b. Hamm   d. Wheezy

Did you know?

The clock on the wall of Andy's room has a hidden
Mickey.

---

37. Which of these is *not* one of the items that assist
    Buzz Lightyear during his flight?
    a. Luxo ball   c. Slinky Dog
    b. Toy airplane   d. Toy car

38. What does Andy use as an antenna on his card-
    board helmet?
    a. Coat hanger   c. A screwdriver
    b. Spatula   d. PVC pipe

39. What do the toys use as a weight when they work
    out with Buzz Lightyear?
    a. Wooden puzzle   c. Toy blocks
       pieces   d. Tinker toys
    b. Lincoln logs

40. When Woody wakes up in the toy box, which toy
    is wearing his hat?
    a. Mr. Potato Head   c. Squeaky shark
    b. Rex   d. Hamm

41. When Buzz asks for the unit directional bonding strip, what is he referring to?
    a. Duct tape   c. White glue
    b. Scotch tape   d. Superglue

42. Where did the toys think Sid was when he returns home?
    a. Visiting grandma c. Summer camp
    b. School   d. Ran away from home

43. What is the first toy Sid blows up with his explosives?
    a. Text and Spell c. Baby Doll
    b. I.G. Joe   d. Combat Carl

44. What is the name of Sid's dog?
    a. Scud   c. Scar
    b. Spud   d. Spike

45. What is the name of the real estate company selling Andy's home?
    a. Lassiter Realty c. Virtual Realty
    b. Pixar Realty   d. Brad Bird Realty

46. What is the answer Woody gets when he asks the Magic 8-ball a question?
    a. Without a doubt c. Reply hazy
    b. Don't count on it d. My reply is no

47. Which object in Andy's room knocks Buzz Lightyear out the window?
    a. Desk lamp   c. RC car
    b. Globe   d. Bulletin board

48. What does Mr. Potato Head draw on the etch a sketch and show to Woody?
    a. A gun   c. Open grave
    b. Guillotine   d. Gallows

Did you know?

The car's license plate reads A113, the animators at Pixar attended the California Institute of the Arts, and A113 is the classroom number for graphic design and character animation.

49. What does Buzz Lightyear has stuck to his face when he falls into the car from the sunroof?
    a. Trash   c. A bug
    b. A leaf   d. A snail

Did you know?

As Buzz and Woody argue about Buzz being a toy, Buzz holds up the Vulcan signal for Live Long and Prosper as he walks away from Woody.

50. How do Buzz and Woody get to Pizza Planet from the gas station?
    a. Hitchhike
    b. Eighteen-wheeler
    c. Walk
    d. Pizza Planet truck

51. What does the back of the Pizza Planet truck say?
    a. Toy
    b. Yo
    c. Toyota
    d. Oy

52. What is the name on the box Buzz hides in to sneak into Pizza Planet?
    a. Super Nova Burger
    b. Galactic Fries
    c. Mega Gulp
    d. Planetary Pizza

53. What is the score on the Planet Killer game inside Pizza Planet?
    a. 6,530,378
    b. 721,342
    c. 6,378, 531
    d. 10,000,000

54. What is the video game next to Whack -A- Alien at Pizza Planet?
    a. Planet Killer
    b. Kabookey
    c. Black Hole
    d. Tron

55. Who is in charge of the Space Crane Game, according to the Alien toys?
    a. Sid
    b. Buzz Lightyear
    c. The aliens
    d. The claw

56. As the Aliens thwart Woody's attempt to save Buzz from being chosen, what does Woody call the Aliens?
    a. Extremists   c. Zealots
    b. Fanatics   d. Maniacs

57. What toy does Sid give to his dog Scud?
    a. Alien   c. Woody
    b. Buzz   d. Baby Doll

58. What is the name of Sid's sister in *Toy Story*?
    a. Emily   c. Hannah
    b. Janey   d. Bonnie

59. What is the time on the wall clock in Sid's room?
    a. 9:38   c. 8:32
    b. 7:47   d. 10:17

60. What comes out of the Jack in the Box in Sid's room?
    a. A foot   c. A spider
    b. A baby doll head   d. A hand

61. As the toys come out to save the doll, what does Buzz call them?
    a. Aliens   c. Mutants
    b. Savages   d. Cannibals

62. What is the name of the cat in the bush as Rex looks for Buzz Lightyear?
    a. Mittens   c. Bambi
    b. Whiskers   d. Sprinkles

> *Did you know?*
>
> The tools Sid uses to mutilate toys are Binford. This is the same tool brand used in the Tim Allen television series *Home Improvement*.

63. What does Woody dunk his head into when Sid burns him with the magnifying glass?
    - a. Bowl of soup
    - b. Glass of water
    - c. Bowl of milk
    - d. Glass of soda

64. What famous line does Woody utter when escaping from Sid's house?
    - a. Say hello to my little friend
    - b. To Infinity and Beyond
    - c. Tomorrow is another day
    - d. There's no place like home

> *Did you know?*
>
> The carpet used in Sid's home is the same pattern as the carpet used in the hotel in *The Shining*.

65. What disclaimer is on the Buzz Lightyear commercial?
    - a. For Ages 3 and up
    - b. Batteries Not Included
    - c. Not a Flying Toy
    - d. Some Assembly Required

66. What sport is Sid's dad watching when he falls asleep in the chair?
    a. Bowling
    b. Hockey
    c. Baseball
    d. Football

67. What name does Hannah give to Buzz while having a tea party?
    a. Mrs. Morris
    b. Mrs. Jones
    c. Mrs. Smith
    d. Mrs. Nesbit

68. What game do Mr. Potato Head and Hamm play?
    a. Battleship
    b. Mousetrap
    c. Monopoly
    d. Parcheesi

69. What does Woody think Sid's toys are going to do to him and Buzz?
    a. Help them
    b. Eat them
    c. Dismantle them
    d. Hide from them

70. Which toy is Mr. Potato Head's moving buddy?
    a. Bo Peep
    b. Slinky Dog
    c. Hamm
    d. Rex

71. What does Woody use to outline the plan to save Buzz to Sid's toys?
    a. Domino's
    b. Checkers
    c. Chess Pieces
    d. Playing Cards

72. What object does Sid set Buzz Lightyear on to shoot off the rocket?
    a. Birdbath
    b. Grill
    c. Plywood
    d. Dartboard

73. What does Sid put in Woody's gun holster?
    a. Match
    b. Gun
    c. Fire Cracker
    d. Rock

74. What song is playing inside the van when the toys are trying to get into the moving van?
    a. It's a Small World
    b. Beauty and the Beast
    c. You've got a Friend in Me
    d. Hakuna Matata

75. Which toy does R.C.'s car hit when he flies into the moving van?
    a. Rex
    b. Mr. Potato Head
    c. Bo Peep
    d. Slinky Dog

76. Which toy holds the mistletoe for Bo Peep when she approaches Woody?
    a. Hamm
    b. Rex
    c. Her sheep
    d. Slinky Dog

77. What does Andy get for Christmas at the end of *Toy Story*?
    a. Mrs. Potato Head
    b. A Puppy
    c. A Video Game,
    d. Zurg action figure

A Bug's Life

78. What sort of bug is the queen's pet?
    a. Aphid
    b. Ladybug
    c. Spider
    d. Ant

79. What is the queen's crown made from?
    a. Sunflower
    b. Pansy
    c. Goldenrod
    d. Daisy

80. What does Flik use as a telescope lens?
    a. Waterdrop
    b. Glass
    c. Sand
    d. Rock

81. What inspired the names on the boxes in the city?
    a. The writers
    b. The writer's children
    c. The director
    d. The voice actors

Did you know?

The number A113 can be seen on one of the cardboard boxes as Flik walks by as he explores the city.

82. What knocked the food off the offering stone?
    a. The ants   c. The grasshoppers
    b. An earthquake   d. Flik's invention

83. Why do the ants agree to send Flik off the island?
    a. To find bigger   c. To find food
       bugs   d. To find a new
    b. To get him out of   place to live.
       the way

84. What does Flik use to get across the gorge?
    a. Grass   c. A Dandelion
    b. A daisy   d. His invention

85. Which is *not* one of the circus performers?
    a. Ladybug   c. Spider
    b. Fly   d. Snail

86. What is the gong in the circus made of?
    a. A Chinese coin   c. A quarter
    b. A penny   d. A dime

87. What does Flik think the circus performers are?
    a. Travelers   c. Food gatherers
    b. Circus bugs   d. Warriors

88. What is written on the homeless bug's sign?
    a. Grasshoppers   c. Homeless, please
       took my home   help
    b. Will work for   d. Kids ripped my
       food   wings off

89. What are used as tables in the bar?
    a. Buttons   c. Spools
    b. Bottle caps   d. Coins

90. What type of blood does the mosquito order?
    a. O+   c. O-
    b. AB   d. B

91. What does ladybug use as a weapon with the flies?
    a. Knife   c. Twig
    b. Walking Stick   d. Antenna

92. What do the performers think Flik is?
    a. A theater owner   c. A talent scout
    b. Manager   d. A famous actor

93. What do the ants use as drums?
    a. Hollow logs   c. Rocks
    b. Seeds   d. Snail shells

94. What show did the ants put on last year?
    a. *Our Town*   c. *A Streetcar*
    b. *Picnic*   *Named Desire*
                           d. *The Glass*
                           Menagerie

95. What are the bugs more afraid of than grasshoppers?
    a. Fish
    b. Humans
    c. Birds
    d. Mosquitos

96. Which bug is made honorary den mother?
    a. Ladybug
    b. Walking stick
    c. Spider
    d. Praying Mantis

Toy Story II

97. What is printed on the monitor Zurg is using to watch Buzz Lightyear navigate his underground bunker?
    a. Playskool
    b. Panavision
    c. Mattel
    d. Zurg Vision

98. As Buzz Lightyear reaches for the source of Zurg's power, what is the item enclosed in the force field?
    a. An electrical cord
    b. A battery
    c. A wall socket
    d. A wind-up key

> **Did you know?**
>
> As Rex plays the video game, there is a wall calendar behind him. The picture shown for August is a reference to *A Bug's Life*, another Pixar film released in 1998.

99. What children's game is underneath the chest of drawers Woody was searching through when he falls to the floor?
    - a. Checkers
    - b. Marbles
    - c. Jacks
    - d. Pick up Sticks

100. As Woody tells Buzz what needs to be done while he is gone, everyone needs to attend the seminar on what to do if part of it is _____.
    - a. Missing
    - b. Swallowed
    - c. Broken
    - d. Stolen

101. As Woody is trying to find his hat, Buzz tells him in a few hours, they will be sitting by a campfire, making what?
    - a. Shmoes
    - b. Shoes
    - c. Smooches
    - d. Graham cracker thingy's

102. When Hamm uses Morse Code to message next door, who tells him it is not in his yard?
    - a. Lawn gnome
    - b. Ceramic goose
    - c. Dog's toy
    - d. Headless barbie

103. What is Mr. Potato Head's endearment for Mrs. Potato Head?
    a. Au Gratin
    b. Baked potato
    c. French fry
    d. Sweet potato

Did you know?

As Mrs. Potato Head reads to the little people, the picture on the page is a scene from *A Bug's Life*.

104. As the commercial for Al's Toy Barn plays on the television, finish this part of the dollar bill in the commercial, "E Pluribus _____."
    a. Moola
    b. Chicken
    c. Toy store
    d. Alfred

105. How many little green army men try to hold the door to Andy's room to keep Buster out?
    a. Twelve
    b. Fifteen
    c. Fourteen
    d. Twenty-four

106. What toy is Mr. and Mrs. Potato Head hiding when Buster is destroying Andy's room?
    a. Tinker toys
    b. Lincoln Logs
    c. Video game box
    d. Barbie dreamhouse

107. How long did it take Buster to find Woody, according to Speak and Spell?
     a. Seven and a half seconds
     b. Twelve and a half seconds
     c. Thirty-five seconds
     d. Thirteen and a half seconds

108. During Woody's nightmare, he is thrown into a trashcan full of what?
     a. Toy arms
     b. Toy legs
     c. Games pieces
     d. Doll heads

109. Which of these is *not* one of the toys on the high shelf where Woody sits in Andy's room?
     a. Yo-Yo
     b. Magic Eight Ball
     c. Stretch Armstrong
     d. Stacking rings

110. What is the name of the penguin toy Woody finds on the high shelf?
     a. Squeaky
     b. Wheezy
     c. Goulet
     d. Robert

111. What object does Woody hide behind at the yard sale during his rescue mission?
   a. Candlestick   c. Teapot
   b. Peppermill   d. Lamp

112. What object does Al offer Andy's mom for Woody?
   a. His wallet   c. His watch
   b. His car   d. His glasses

113. As Buzz makes his way across the yard to save Woody from Al, what does the bottom of the yard sale sign say?
   a. No early birds   c. Saturday only
   b. No negotiating   d. All offers
                          welcome

114. What does the vanity plate on Al's car read?
   a. LZYTBAN   c. LSTYBRN
   b. ALZTBRN   d. LZTYBRN

115. When Al opens the glass door to his apartment, what is not allowed in the building?
   a. Solicitors   c. Children
   b. Toys   d. Teenagers

116. Which board game box does Hamm stand on to show the exhibits to the rest of the toys?
   a. Clue   c. Candyland
   b. Life   d. Scrabble

117. When Jessie meets Woody, she exclaims, "Sweet mother of _____."

    a. Martin Luther King
    b. Roy Rogers
    c. George Washington
    d. Abraham Lincoln

118. Which of these is *not* one of the sayings on Stinky Pete's box?

    a. There's gold in them thar hills
    b. My ax is my best friend
    c. Help! I think I'm stuck
    d. Oh Boy!...Beans for dinner

Did you know?

The scarf the Stinky Pete wears is the same pattern as Woody's shirt.

119. What is the name of the cereal that sponsors Woody's Roundup?

    a. Cowboy Crunchies
    b. Cowboy Flakes
    c. Cowboy Lassos
    d. Roundup Rings

Did you know?

When Woody reads the cover of LIFE magazine, Jan. 12, 1957, is John Lasseter's birthday.

120. According to the cover of LIFE magazine, what is it that American's do not eat enough of?
    a. Vegetables   c. Sugar
    b. Fat   d. Beef

121. What is the time on the VCR that Bullseye inserts the video cassette into read?
    a. 8:14   c. 3:45
    b. 5:27   d. 12:00

Did you know?

As Hamm speeds through the television channels, you can catch glimpses of several Pixar short cartoons.

Did you know?

Al's Toy Barn's address is 1001 W. Cutting Blvd, and this is Pixar Studios' address in Richmond, California.

122. As Woody rides to save Stinky Pete and Jessie on Woody's Roundup, what does he and Bullseye jump over on the way to the old abandoned mine shaft?
    a. The Grand   c. The Atlantic
       Canyon   Ocean
    b. Mount Everest   d. The moon

123. What event canceled Woody's Roundup, according to Stinky Pete?
    a. The moon landing
    b. Sputnik
    c. The berlin wall coming down
    d. The Vietnam war

124. What is written on the side of the barrel on the Woody penny bank?
    a. Woody
    b. Bank
    c. Savings
    d. Orphans

125. How many blocks in total do the toys need to go to get to Al's Toy Barn?
    a. Nineteen
    b. Twenty-one
    c. Two
    d. Ninety

126. What does Bullseye do that could wake Al while he sleeps on the couch?
    a. Turns on the television
    b. Steps on the snacks
    c. Licks his fingers
    d. Starts the record player

127. Where does Bullseye hide while Jessie beats up Woody?
    a. Cookie jar
    b. Cardboard box
    c. Behind the record player
    d. In a drawer

128. How much change is Hamm carrying while the toys make their way to Al's Toy Barn?
    a. Seventy-two cents
    b. Twelve dollars
    c. Seventeen dollars
    d. Over six dollars

129. What do the toys use to safely cross the street to get to Al's Toy Barn?
    a. Garbage
    b. Pipes
    c. Road cones
    d. Crosswalk

Did you know?

The elderly gentleman that comes to restore Woody is the same character from the Pixar short Geri's Game! In which the man plays chess with himself in the park. As he opens the drawers of his kit, you will see a glimpse of a chess piece in one of the drawers.

Did you know?

As the restoration artist opens the drawer of eyes, the eyes create a hidden Mickey.

130. Which of these is *not* one of the items revealed in the drawers of the restoration kit?
    a. Arms
    b. Voice boxes
    c. Eyeballs
    d. Chess pieces

Did you know?

As Buzz Lightyear runs through the toy story, there is Bugs' display from *A Bug's Life* on the end cap of one of the aisles.

131. Which code did Buzz direct is violation over according to the Buzz Lightyear on display?
    a. 8146.0
    b. 4606.5
    c. 5404.6
    d. 6404.5

132. What is Barbie cooking on the grill when the toy finds the pool party?
    a. Steak
    b. Fish
    c. Corn
    d. Chicken

133. What is the name of the song that is playing during the pool party at the toy store?
    a. Surfin' U.S.A.
    b. Wipe Out
    c. California Girls
    d. Itsy Bitsy Teeny Weenie Yellow Polka-dot Bikini

134. According to Tour Guide Barbie, how many cars were included in the original 1967 Hot Wheels™ set?
    a. Sixteen cars
    b. Fifteen cars
    c. Seventeen cars
    d. Twenty-six cars

135. When the magazine Rex reads slides beneath the store shelves, what game is on the bottom shelf priced at $7.99?
    a. Hungry Hungry Horses
    b. Don't Eat the Jalapenos
    c. Rat Trap
    d. Scribble

Did you know?

As Rex chases the blue car through the toy store, the animators pay homage to *Jurassic Park* when Mr. Potato Head looks in the side view mirror to see Rex catching up to the car.

Did you know?

When the car stops abruptly, and Rex falls over into the back seat, Barbie utters, "Remain Seated Please, permanecen sentados, por favor." This is part of the safety script for rides at Disneyland and Walt Disney World.

136. What color is the bicycle resting against the truck at the donation site where Jessie is left?
    a. Black
    b. Red
    c. Green
    d. Blue

137. What was the name of the girl who owned Jessie?
    a. Emily
    b. Mary
    c. Sarah
    d. Brooke

138. As Slinky Dog talks to the Rock 'Em Sock 'Em Robots, read the bulletin board behind them. What aisle does Al need to restock?
    a. Barbie
    b. Buzz Lightyear
    c. Games
    d. Hot Wheels

139. What is the price of the Pummel the Clown toy that Buzz hides behind to follow Al?
    a. $12.99
    b. $7.99
    c. $21.99
    d. $16.99

140. When the toys are attempting to exit Al's car, what does Mr. Potato Head call Rex when he unlocks the car door?
    a. Barney
    b. Godzilla
    c. Chomper
    d. Dinohead

141. When Hamm recommends they deliver a ham sandwich with fries and a hot dog, what does he suggest Rex do to help?
    a. Stand guard
    b. Be the delivery dinosaur
    c. Lay down in the sandwich
    d. Be the toy that comes with the meal

142. When Wood, Jessie, and Stinky Pete are dancing, what does Stinky Pete say he is doing?
    a. The do si do
    b. The box step
    c. The two-step
    d. The foxtrot

143. As the toys are climbing the elevator shaft, which toy says his arms are giving out?
    a. Hamm
    b. Rex
    c. Mr. Potato Head
    d. Slinky Dog

144. When the toys find Woody, what do they think Jessie and Bullseye are doing to woody?
    a. Torturing him
    b. Kidnapping him
    c. Beating him up
    d. Force-feeding him

145. What does Mr. Potato Head put on his eye sockets when he states, "Get ready to meet Mr. Angry Eyes?"
    a. Eyes
    b. Feet
    c. Ears
    d. A nose

146. When the real Buzz catches up with the toy store Buzz, what is the code he tells the toy story Buzz?
    a. 465
    b. 654
    c. 546
    d. 564

147. As the toys leave Woody to go back to Andy's house, who looks back at Woody one last time before leaving?
    a. Buzz
    b. Hamm
    c. Rex
    d. Slinky Dog

148. What does Woody sit down on to watch Woody's Roundup after his friends leave?
    a. A marker
    b. A roll of packing tape
    c. A book
    d. A packing peanut

149. What does Stinky Pete use to tighten the screws on the air vent to stop Woody from leaving?
    a. A pen
    b. A screwdriver
    c. His pickaxe
    d. A paperclip

150. Where did Stinky Peter spend years watching other toys be sold?
    a. Dime store
    b. Toy store
    c. Second-hand store
    d. Antique store

151. As Al returns and packs Woody for shipping, what snack does he take with him?
    a. Corn nuts
    b. Cheese puffs
    c. Beef Jerky
    d. Salt and vinegar chips

152. When the toys are ambushed by Zurg at the elevator shaft, what does Rex call his weapon?
    a. Ion blaster
    b. Lightsaber
    c. Foam blaster
    d. Zapper

153. Who does Rex land on when he lands on top of the elevator?
    a. Mr. Potato Head
    b. Slinky Dog
    c. Hamm
    d. Buzz

> *Did you know?*
>
> When Zurg reveals he is Buzz Lightyears father, this is another reference to Star Wars: The Empire Strikes Back when Luke falls after Darth Vader reveals this to him.

154. How do the toys stop the front door of the apartment building from shutting?
    - a. Buzz Lightyears utility belt
    - b. Slinky Dog's butt
    - c. Mr. Potato Head's angry eyes
    - d. Mr. Potato Head's hat

> *Did you know?*
>
> The toys use the Pizza Planet Truck from Toy Story to get them to the airport.

155. As the toys commandeer the Pizza Planet Truck, what do the aliens call the stick shift?
    - a. Wand of direction
    - b. Wand of transport
    - c. Wand of power
    - d. Wand of destiny

156. When the carrier holding the toys goes to the luggage area, Slinky has a sticker with LHR on his face; what do these letters mean?
    - a. Heathrow Airport
    - b. Aeroport La Rochelle
    - c. Valley International Airport
    - d. Lawrence and Hansen Airport

> *Did you know?*
>
> When Stinky Pete lands on the luggage carousel, the announcement for Lassiter Air flight A113 arriving from Richmond can be heard. This is a nod to producer John Lassiter and A113 for the classroom at Cal Arts and the city where Pixar is headquartered.

157. When Hamm changes the television channel, what sticker is attached to the side of the screen ?
     a. Cowboy hat   c. Footprints
     b. Rainbow   d. Planet

158. Who helped Wheezy find a new squeaker in the toy box?
     a. Green army men   c. Firemen
     b. Mr. Shark   d. Binoculars

> *Did you know?*
>
> During the credits, the animators created outtakes as if the animated characters made bloopers like real live actors.

Monster's Inc.

159. What is the time on the alarm clock in the simulator at the beginning of *Monster's Inc.*?
   a. 4:50
   c. 5:04
   b. 4:05
   d. 9:04

160. What kind of ball is under the bed of the Simulator?
   a. Baseball
   c. Basketball
   b. Football
   d. Soccer

161. When the simulation is over, what does the first monster say his friends call him?
   a. Fungus
   c. Phlegm
   b. Mucus
   d. Ooze

Did you know?

As the simulation controller rewinds the tape, the number on the display next to the dial is the Pixar studios' phone number.

162. How many eyes does Mr. Waternoose have?
    a. Five   c. Nine
    b. Six   d. Twelve

163. What is the scream capacity of each canister used in Monsters Inc.?
    a. 10,000 SUV   c. 8,400 SUV
    b. 2,400 SUV   d. 8,500 SUV

164. How does Mike wake Sulley for work?
    a. Air Horn   c. Shakes Him
    b. Alarm Clock   d. Tickles Him

> *Did you know?*
>
> As Sulley works out, the chair behind him in the living room has a hole cut out for his tail.

165. As Mike trains Sulley for work, what object does he attach the drawing of the child's face to?
    a. Shovel   c. Mop
    b. Rake   d. Broom

166. How many crunches does Sulley do hanging from the ceiling?
    a. One hundred   c. Fifty
    b. One hundred   d. Two hundred
       twenty

167. What is the name of the monster Sulley recognizes in the commercial for Monsters Inc.?
    a. Susie
    b. Mary
    c. Betty
    d. Tammy

168. Who calls the house after the television commercial?
    a. Rex
    b. Mike's mom
    c. Mr. Waternoose
    d. Sulley's mom

169. What is the name of the newspaper in Monstropolis?
    a. Monstropolis Horn
    b. Monstropolis Times
    c. Monstropolis Gazette
    d. Monstropolis Journal

Did you know?

Mike and Sulley walk past the Hidden City Café on their way to work. This store pays homage to the real Hidden City Café in Richmond, California, the headquarters of Pixar.

Did you know?

On the back wall of the Hidden City Café, there is a poster for the Storybook Land Canal Boats at Disneyland. It can be seen through the glass in the front door.

170. As Mike and Sulley walk past Tony's Grossery, which product is $4.299 according to the advertisement on the window?
    a. Mangle fruit
    b. Blood oranges
    c. Bilge berries
    d. Flea dip

171. If you look at the Employee of the month pictures in the lobby of Monsters Inc., how many months has Sulley been an employee of the month?
    a. Ten
    b. Eleven
    c. Twelve
    d. Six

Did you know?

When Mike opens his locker at the factory, several Post-It notes remind him to file his paperwork.

172. What is the advertisement on the back of the paper Roz is reading?
    a. Weight loss
    b. Fang sharpening
    c. Fur replacement
    d. Claw removal

173. What is the number of the first card key Mike swipes for Sulley?
    a. 13089
    b. 19308
    c. 19038
    d. 13098

174. How many scaring stations are there on the scare floor?
    a. Thirteen
    b. Twelve
    c. Eleven
    d. Ten

> **Did you know?**
>
> As Randall prepares for his scare day, one of the backdrops his assistant pulls down is the wallpaper from Andy's room in *Toy Story*.

175. How many eyes does the purple monster place on his face to prepare for his scare day?
    a. Twenty-seven   c. Fifteen
    b. Seventeen   d. Sixteen

176. What is Randall's scare total at the beginning of the day?
    a. 99,479   c. 79,012
    b. 99,351   d. 10,000

> **Did you know?**
>
> Some of the names on the scare totals board are the animators' names who worked on *Monster Inc.*

> **Did you know?**
>
> When the blue monster comes out of the child's room immediately after Randall, there is a poster for the Rocket Jets ride at Disneyland on the child's wall.

177. How long has does Mr. Waternoose say it's been since they met their quota?
    a. One year   c. One month
    b. One week   d. Six months

178. How many doors have they lost this week?
    a. Fifty-eight   c. One hundred
    b. Seventy-eight   eight
                         d. Eight

179. How do they destroy old doors?
    a. Garbage pile   c. Shredder
    b. Burning   d. Sledge hammer

180. What object is found on George Sanderson when he has a 2319?
    a. Glove   c. Scarf
    b. Sock   d. Shoe

181. How many days was the scare floor accident-free before the reset?
    a. Ten   c. Seventy-four
    b. Forty-seven   d. Twenty-three

182. What number is on Sulley's locker?
    a. 347   c. 351
    b. 360   d. 374

183. Where is Mike taking Celia after dinner?
    a. The movies
    b. Monster dancing
    c. Monster truck rally
    d. Driving in his car

184. Which is *not* one of the odorants Sulley offers Mike?
    a. Rotting Food
    b. Old Dumpster
    c. Wet Dog
    d. Smelly garbage

185. Which is *not* one of the form colors on Mike's paperwork?
    a. Puce
    b. Goldenrod
    c. Fuchsia
    d. Teal

186. How does Sulley try to get rid of the items from Boo's bedroom?
    a. Put them back
    b. Throw in the trash
    c. Flush them
    d. Take them Home

187. What is Boo's nickname for Sulley?
    a. Kitty
    b. Pretty
    c. Sulley
    d. Puppy

188. What kind of food is served at Harryhausen's?
    a. Sushi
    b. Italian
    c. Szechuan
    d. Cantonese

> *Did you know?*
>
> Harryhausen's is a tribute to Academy Award™ artist Harry Hausen. Hausen was a pioneer of stop motion animation and visual effects.

> *Did you know?*
>
> There is a fish design behind the sushi chef of Nemo from *Finding Nemo*.

189. What is Sulley wearing on his head to protect himself from Boo?
    - a. Helmet
    - b. Cooking Pot
    - c. Colander
    - d. Cereal Bowl

190. What is the name of Mike's bear?
    - a. Mr. Bear
    - b. Little Mikey
    - c. Shmootsy Poo
    - d. Ted

191. What food does Sulley feed Boo while she is coloring?
    - a. Cookies
    - b. Crackers
    - c. Spaghetti
    - d. Cereal

192. Which of these is *not* one of the options Mike comes up with to get rid of Boo?
    - a. Giant wooden horse
    - b. Drive it into the country
    - c. Dig a tunnel under the city
    - d. Giant slingshot

> **Did you know?**
>
> When Boo crawls into Sulley's bed, the molding on the wall around his bed makes a hidden Mickey.

193. Who is Boo's monster?
     - a. Sulley
     - b. Randall
     - c. Mike
     - d. George

194. What does Sulley use to sit on when he guards the closet door for Boo so she will fall asleep?
     - a. A bean bag chair
     - b. Cinder blocks
     - c. A spool
     - d. A chair

> **Did you know?**
>
> As Sulley takes Boo to the restroom in the factory, there is a clear hidden Mickey in the purple spots on his left leg.

195. What does Mike tell the other workers they need when he makes up the company play?
     - a. Background actors
     - b. Concession workers
     - c. Ushers
     - d. Lighting techs

196. When Randall gives Mike hints that the scare floor will be empty, what is Mike's first guess?
    a. The scare floor will be carpeted
    b. The scare floor will be fumigated
    c. The scare floor will be cleaned
    d. The scare floor will be painted

197. Why does the CDA stop Sulley in the hallway of the factory?
    a. Scare demonstration
    b. Interrogation
    c. Autograph
    d. Picture

198. What name does the CDA tell Sulley to make the autograph out to?
    a. Stephanie
    b. Trixie
    c. Telly
    d. Brian

199. What does Boo tell the daycare lady her name is?
    a. Sulley
    b. Boo
    c. Kitty
    d. Mike Wazowski

200. Who does Randall accidentally kidnap and take to his secret hideout?
    a. Roz
    b. Boo
    c. Sulley
    d. Mike

201. What time is it when Randall puts Boo's door in the station?
    a. Quitting time
    b. Dinner
    c. Lunch
    d. Midnight

202. When Randall straps Mike into the scream extractor and the machine fails, what does Fungus' guess could be wrong?
    a. Hydraulic scream lever
    b. Scream intake valve
    c. Mechanical scream hose
    d. Scream vacuum tube

203. What does Mike bribe Fungus with to let him go?
    a. Money
    b. His car
    c. A ride in his car
    d. He won't tell

204. Where do Mike & Sulley get banished from Monstropolis?
    a. The Himalayas
    b. Loch Ness
    c. The bayou
    d. Paris

205. Who do Mike and Sulley find when they get banished?
    a. Godzilla
    b. Big Foot
    c. Loch Ness monster
    d. Abominable snowman

206. As the Abominable Snowman talks to Mike about his name, what is on the wooden box label near his feet?
    a. Boysenberry
    b. Lingonberry
    c. Serviceberries
    d. Chokeberries

207. What flavor snow cones does the Abominable Snowman offer Mike & Sulley?
    a. Cherry   c. Blueberry
    b. Lemon   d. Grape

208. What did Big Foot call himself after he was banished?
    a. Yeti   c. King Scratchy
    b. Sasquatch   d. King Itchy

209. What does the Abominable Snowman tell Mike and Sulley they can get for free in the nearby village?
    a. Yak's meat   c. Yak's milk
    b. Goat's milk   d. Flax milk

210. As Mike and Sulley ride the door to get away from Randall, Finish Mike's line, "What a plan. simple yet _____."
    a. Crazy   c. Impossible
    b. Elegant   d. Insane

211. Which of these is *not* one of the places Mike and Sulley find when opening the various doors?
    a. Mexico   c. Tahiti
    b. Japan   d. Paris

212. Which of these is *not* one of the patterns created on Randall when Boo beats him up?
    a. Argyle   c. Flowers
    b. Polka dots   d. Bricks

> **Did you know?**
>
> The trailer and Pizza Planet truck are the same set used in *A Bug's Life*.

213. When Mike produces the white sock and throws it on the CDA member, what is the CDA member's number?
     a. 00002
     c. 01196
     b. 82472
     d. 01040

214. Who is the head of the CDA?
     a. Roz
     c. Mr. Waternoose
     b. Celia
     d. Randall

215. What is Boo's real name?
     a. Tilly
     c. Maria
     b. Kelly
     d. Mary

> **Did you know?**
>
> The Luxo ball is sitting on the floor in Boo's bedroom. Boo also hands Sulley a clownfish, which hints at the next Pixar film, *Finding Nemo*.

216. What Pixar character toy does Boo hand to Sulley when she gets home?
     a. Buzz Lightyear
     c. Woody
     b. Jessie
     d. Bullseye

> *Did you know?*
>
> The white chair in the corner of Boo's bedroom has a hidden Mickey carved into one of the slats.

217. When Mike is doing his stand-up routine in the child's bedroom, how many years does he say he was in kindergarten?
   - a. Two
   - b. Three
   - c. Five
   - d. Seven

218. What is the name on the soccer team poster in the child's room that Mike performs in?
   - a. Glow sticks
   - b. Colts
   - c. Bandits
   - d. Cowboys

219. What is the name of the magazine Mike and Sulley appear on?
   - a. Monsters Inc. Magazine
   - b. Newshriek
   - c. Peoples
   - d. Business Shriek

> *Did you know?*
>
> One of the monsters walks across the floor carrying a watermelon and a wooden mallet. This is a tribute to Watermelon smasher Gallagher.

220. What does Sulley keep to remember Boo?
   - a. Toy
   - b. Drawing
   - c. Photograph
   - d. Her Costume

Did you know?

At the end of the credits, a disclaimer says, "No monsters were harmed in the making of this motion picture."

Finding Nemo

221. How many children do Coral and Marlin have?
    a. Over four hundred
    b. Over five hundred
    c. Over one hundred
    d. Over four thousand

222. What kind of home does Nemo live in?
    a. Coral
    b. Anemone
    c. A rock
    d. A sunken ship

223. What line did Marlin use when he met Coral?
    a. Is there a hook in my lip?
    b. Do you work at the fish and bait shop?
    c. You look like a fish I've seen before
    d. Didn't our kids go to the same school?

224. What does Marlin call Nemo's small fin?
    a. Small fin
    b. Tiny Fin
    c. Gimpy Fin
    d. Lucky Fin

225. How does Marlin tell if Nemo has a break?
     a. Feels like coral
     b. Crunching noise
     c. Fluid rushing
     d. Smells like eel

226. What is the name of the kid who tells Nemo how old sea turtles are?
     a. Cindy Plankton
     b. Sandy Plankton
     c. Sandy Plimpton
     d. Stanley Plankton

227. When Marlin freaked out at the petting zoo, which animal was ready to charge?
     a. Starfish
     b. Sea cucumber
     c. Snail
     d. Seahorse

228. Where does Marlin tell Nemo to play?
     a. The sponge bed
     b. The drop-off
     c. Mr. Johansson's yard
     d. At home

229. Which is *not* one of Nemo's friends?
     a. Seahorse
     b. Octopus
     c. Fish
     d. Shrimp

230. As Mr. Ray takes the class, he tells them to keep what part of their body to themselves?
     a. Supraesophageal ganglion
     b. Anoplogaster cornuta
     c. Enypniastes eximia
     d. Psychrolutes microporos

231. What happens to Pearl when she gets scared?
    a. She screams   c. She inks
    b. She cries   d. She falls over

Did you know?

The camera the diver uses is model A113. This is a reference to the classroom at Cal Arts, where the Pixar animators studied their craft.

Did you know?

As Marlin goes to the surface of the water to try to locate the boat, he goes back under the water to get another breath of air.

232. What does Dory struggle with?
    a. Patrial blindness   c. Short term
    b. Directions   memory loss
                              d. Gimpy Fin

233. What is the name of the shark Marlin and Dory meet?
    a. Jaws   c. Bruiser
    b. Bruce   d. Spike

234. What object does Dory call Balloons?
    a. Anchors   c. Life preservers
    b. Buoys   d. Mines

235. Where does Bruce take Marlin and Dory?
    a. A recovery meeting
    b. A barbeque
    c. A funeral
    d. A revival meeting

236. What step are the sharks on in their recovery?
    a. Step four
    b. Step five
    c. Step eight
    d. Step twelve

237. What does Bruce use as a podium in the sunken submarine?
    a. Clipboard
    b. Ships wheel
    c. Sink
    d. Radio

238. How long has it been since Bruce's last fish?
    a. Three years
    b. Two weeks
    c. Three months
    d. Three weeks

239. What is the deep dark secret Bruce reveals at the meeting?
    a. He always wanted to dance
    b. He dropped out of school
    c. He never knew his father
    d. He secretly loves seaweed

240. What causes Bruce to chase Marlin and Dory?
    a. Bloody nose
    b. He gets hungry
    c. Peer pressure
    d. He goes fishing

241. Where do Marlin and Dory hide from Bruce?
    a. Ship
    b. Submarine compartment
    c. Cave
    d. Coral Reef

Did you know?

As Bruce chases Marlin and Dory through the submarine, he breaks open part of a door. Bruce quotes *The Shining* when he peeks his head in and says, "Here's Brucey."

Did you know?

There is a Buzz Lightyear toy on the floor at the dentist's office by the toy chest.

---

242. What is the name of the dentist's assistant?
    a. Darla
    b. Sheila
    c. Tina
    d. Barbara

243. Who does Nemo meet first when he is dropped in the fish tank?
    a. Gurgle
    b. Peach
    c. Bubbles
    d. Jacques

244. As the fish in the aquarium introduce themselves to Nemo, where did the dentist get Peach?
    a. Bob's Fish Market
    b. eBay
    c. Pet Palace
    d. Mail order

245. Where in the aquarium does Jacques live?
    a. Diving helmet
    b. Castle
    c. Coral reef
    d. Treasure chest

246. What kind of file does Bloat say the dentist is using on the root canal?
    a. Endodontic file
    b. K file
    c. Glidden drill
    d. Hedstrom file

247. What kind of creature is Nigel?
    a. Duck
    b. Seagull
    c. Pelican
    d. Pigeon

248. What is Darla's relationship with the dentist?
    a. Daughter
    b. Niece
    c. Granddaughter
    d. Cousin

249. How did Darla kill her last present?
    a. Shook the bag
    b. Flushed him
    c. Forgot to feed
    d. Dropped him

250. What does the sign next to the skull in the fish tank say?
    a. Fish Gotta Swim
    b. Pirates Life
    c. Yo Ho
    d. Didn't brush

Did you know?

As Gil tells the rest of the fish his escape plan, the Pizza Planet truck drives down the street as the bags of fish fall out the dentist's office window.

251. When Dory is dreaming, who has Dory's money?
    a. Sea cucumber   c. Sea slug
    b. Sea monkey   d. Jellyfish

252. What object bears the address 42 Wallaby Way Sydney?
    a. Swim fins   c. Diving mask
    b. Snorkel   d. Camera

253. What does Dory call Marlin after the mask falls to the ocean floor?
    a. Grumpy tail   c. Grumpy gills
    b. Grumpy fins   d. Grumpy stripes

254. When the aquarium's fish offer to let Nemo into their club, what is the ring of fire?
    a. A plastic firepot   c. A blinking light
    b. Plastic plants   d. Bubbles

255. What do the fish in the tank nickname Nemo?
    a. Orange and White   c. Ring of Fire
    b. Shark Bait   d. Jail Bait

Did you know?

As Gil tells Nemo that the tank will get filthy, there is a shot of the mermaid from the Pixar short, Knick Knack at the bow of the ship in the tank.

256. What does Nemo use to jam the filter in the tank?
   - a. Pebble
   - b. Leaf
   - c. Plastic treasure
   - d. Fish food

257. Which of these is *not* one of the shapes the moon-fish take when talking to Marlin and Dory?
   - a. Trench
   - b. Jellyfish
   - c. Swordfish
   - d. Sydney Opera House

> *Did you know?*
>
> When the moonfish create the ship, one of the fish walks the plank at the back of the ship.

258. How long does the moonfish say they will follow the EAC?
   - a. One week
   - b. Three days
   - c. Three months
   - d. Three weeks

259. What sea creature does Dory name Squishy?
   - a. Jellyfish
   - b. Seahorse
   - c. String ray
   - d. Moray eel

> *Did you know?*
>
> Three of the Jellyfish make a hidden Mickey when looking down at the top of them.

260. When Marlin and Dory race out of the Jellyfish, what does he tell Dory to eat?
    a. His dust
    b. His speed
    c. His fin
    d. His bubbles

261. What magazine does the dentist grab when he goes to the bathroom?
    a. Readers Digest
    b. Dentist Quarterly
    c. The Star
    d. Divers Digest

262. What does Crush tell Marlin he has a serious problem with?
    a. Death
    b. Thrills
    c. Anger
    d. Motion sickness

263. When Crush tells Marlin not to hurl on his shell, what is his excuse?
    a. He doesn't want to clean it
    b. Just washed it
    c. Just waxed it
    d. He is squeamish

264. What is Dory doing when Marlin thinks she is sick?
    a. Playing hide and seek
    b. Sleeping
    c. Playing charades
    d. Playing Twister

265. What does Crush call Marlin?
    a. Mini Marlin
    b. Mr. Turtle
    c. Jelly Man
    d. Little Blue

> ### Did you know?
>
> Each of the turtle kids has a different floral pattern on their shells. Each looks like a different Hawaiian flower.

266. What is the lobster's name stuck in the trap as the sea creatures tell Marlin's story?
    a. Luke
    b. John
    c. Mark
    d. Bob

267. What does the sign on the red buoy read where the seagulls are begging for food?
    a. Slow no wake
    b. Treated sewage
    c. No fishing
    d. No boating

268. What does Nigel call the seagulls when he is trying to eat a crab?
    a. Beggars
    b. Vultures
    c. Garbage cans
    d. Rats with wings

269. Whose tooth does the dentist pull when Nigel hits the window?
    a. Senator
    b. President
    c. Prime Minister
    d. Congressman

270. When it is time for Marlin and Dory to exit the EAC, what does he call the exit?
    a. Swirling vortex of terror
    b. Swirling vortex of death
    c. Swirling vortex of danger
    d. Swirling vortex of fear

271. How old is Crush the sea turtle?
    a. Two hundred   c. One hundred
        fifty   fifty
    b. One hundred   d. Five hundred
                                   fifty

272. What language does Dory speak?
    a. Dolphin   c. Swordfish
    b. Whale   d. Jellyfish

273. What shape does Peach make on the dirty tank?
    a. Hollywood   c. Tank angels
        squares   d. Scum angels
    b. Crop circles

274. What is the whale eating when he swallows Marlin and Dory?
    a. Shrimp   c. Krill
    b. Plankton   d. Fish

275. As Dory and Marlin are inside the whale, finish this line, "He either said go to the back of the throat of he wants a _____."
    a. Root beer float   c. Swim in a moat
    b. New fur coat   d. Milk a goat

276. What is the name of the aquarium cleaning system?
    a. Aqua Man   c. Aqua Fresh
    b. Aqua Scum   d. Aqua Tone

277. What is the dentist doing in the photograph next to the fish tank?
    a. Family photo
    b. Getting Married
    c. Receiving an award
    d. Going fishing

278. When the tank cleaning system scans the tank, what is the temperature of the water?
    a. 82 degrees
    b. 28 degrees
    c. 92 degrees
    d. 72 degrees

279. What does Gurgle say in response to the new tank cleaning system?
    a. Doom you
    b. Plague you
    c. Scourge you
    d. Curse you

280. What does the front of Darla's shirt say?
    a. Aussie Girl
    b. Princess
    c. Gone Fishing
    d. Rock N Roll Girl

Did you know?

As Marlin and Dory swim through the harbor, the names on the boats are titles of Pixar short cartoons.

281. What is the name of the seagull who tries to swallow Marlin and Dory?
    a. Nigel
    b. Gerald
    c. Bob
    d. Roger

282. What is the name of the snack shop the Pelican's roost on?
    a. Castaway Cay
    b. Devil's Bayou
    c. Angel's Cove
    d. Gusteau's

283. What song does Darla sing while she taps on the glass of the aquarium?
    a. *Twinkle Twinkle Little Star*
    b. *Old MacDonald*
    c. *Rock a bye baby*
    d. *ABC's*

284. What type of fish does Darla tell her uncle she is?
    a. Clownfish
    b. Piranha
    c. Blue tang
    d. Tigerfish

285. When the dentist thinks Nemo is dead, where does he tell Darla he left her present?
    a. In the car
    b. In his office
    c. At his house
    d. At the fish store

Did you know?

The boy sitting in the dentist waiting room is reading a comic book with The Incredibles on the cover, hinting at one of the next Pixar films.

286. Find the poster on the office wall that says Floss; what animal is on the poster?
    a. Piranha
    b. Whale
    c. Alligator
    d. Shark

287. Which instrument is Nemo laying on when Gil catapults him into the drain?
    a. Water sprayer
    b. Drill
    c. Pick
    d. Mirror

288. What does Nemo call Squirt when he visits his class?
    a. Transfer student
    b. Exchange student
    c. New student
    d. Visitor

289. Which is *not* one of the names Dory calls Nemo?
    a. Harpo
    b. Chico
    c. Fabio
    d. Groucho

290. How does the tank fish escape the dentist's office?
    a. Down the drain
    b. Plastic bags
    c. Pretend to be dead
    d. They do not

Did you know?

During the Special Thanks credits, Mike Wazowski swims through the ocean with a snorkel.

The Incredibles

291. As Mr. Incredible is being interviewed, what does he say he feels like?
    a. The parent
    b. The janitor
    c. The maid
    d. The teacher

292. What is the license plate of the police car chasing the bad guys?
    a. PRYMSN
    b. DRGNET
    c. PTRGUN
    d. KR 54

Did you know?

The license plate on the police car refers to the television show *Car 54, Where Are you?*

293. As Mr. Incredible listens to the report of the police chase, what street is the chase on?
    a. San Maria Ave
    b. San Vicente Ave
    c. San Pablo Ave
    d. San Fernando Ave

294. When Mr. Incredible opens the secret compartment in his car and reveals the map, what is the name of the city directly across the bay from Municiberg?
    a. Desertville
    b. Villaville
    c. Sticksville
    d. Boondock valley

295. When Mr. Incredible zooms in to isolate the pursuit, what street is between West St. and Genoa Street?
    a. Shellmound Ave.
    b. Christie St.
    c. Brockhurst St.
    d. Hollis St.

296. What is the name of the cat Mr. Incredible stops to save while in pursuit of the criminals?
    a. Spike
    b. Binx
    c. Squishy
    d. Squeaker

297. What is the name Mr. Incredible calls Buddy before Incrediboy corrects him?
    a. Brandon
    b. Brady
    c. Brock
    d. Brody

Did you know?

As the thief is going through the purse he has stolen, there is a Mr. Incredible Pez dispenser in the purse.

298. When Mr. Incredible tries to save Buddy from the bomb attached to his cape, what does Buddy say he is wrecking?
    a. His cape flow
    b. His cool escape
    c. His flight pattern
    d. His awesomeness

Did you know?

All of the superheroes in the second row at the wedding are the same heroes who die.

299. What is the last name of the man suing Mr. Incredible for saving his life?
    a. Sanderson
    b. Sansweet
    c. Sandoval
    d. Sansdole

300. What is the form number that Mr. Incredible tells the client to fill out?
    a. WS2475
    b. SW4257
    c. WS5742
    d. SW2475

301. As Mr. Incredibles box leaves his cubicle, what falls off his desk?
    a. Phone
    b. His lunch
    c. Pencil cup
    d. Stapler

302. What is the first name of Dash's teacher?
    a. Billy
    b. Bennie
    c. Benji
    d. Bernie

303. What is Dash's middle name?
    a. Robert
    b. Incredible
    c. Flash
    d. Marion

304. What is the name of the boy Violet has a crush on?
    a. Tim
    b. Bob
    c. Steve
    d. Tony

305. What is the house number of the Parr family?
    a. 113
    b. 440
    c. 26862
    d. 2480

306. What does Dash tell his father about the school to avoid telling him he was called to the office?
    a. Mary Jane threw up
    b. Dissected a frog
    c. He won at dodgeball
    d. Monday is a holiday

307. Which of these is *not* one of the meals for the left-over night?
    a. Meatloaf
    b. Steak
    c. Salmon
    d. Pasta

308. What is the date on the newspaper Mr. Incredible reads in the kitchen?
    a. May 16, 1962
    b. August 14, 1962
    c. December 2, 1989
    d. November 5, 2004

309. What is Lucius's wife's name?
    a. Frozene
    b. Sweetums
    c. Honey
    d. Weezy

310. What is code 2356 when Bob and Lucius are listening to the police scanner?
    a. Cat up a tree
    b. Fire
    c. Kidnapping
    d. Robbery

> **Did you know?**
>
> As Bob and Lucius pull out of the alley to drive to the fire, there is an advertisement on the building for Luxo Deli. This is a nod to the Pixar short Luxo Jr.

> **Did you know?**
>
> When Lucius and Bob are caught in the jewelry store by the police officer, this is a reference to the film *Die Hard with a Vengeance* starring Samuel L. Jackson, the voice of Frozone.

311. What song is Mr. Incredible humming when he gets home from the fire?
    - a. *Beyond the Sea*
    - b. *You've got a Friend in Me*
    - c. *If I Didn't Have You*
    - d. *The Incredibles theme*

312. What does Mrs. Incredible find on her husband's clothes when he gets home?
    - a. A hair
    - b. Rubble
    - c. Smoke
    - d. A diamond

313. When the kids catch their parents arguing, what does Mrs. Incredible tell the kids they are united against?
    - a. Lying
    - b. Evil
    - c. Pigheadedness
    - d. Sneaking around

314. According to Bob's boss, who are the first people they need to help?
    a. The stockholders
    b. The customers
    c. Him
    d. The employees

315. How many walls does Bob throw his boss through when he loses his job?
    a. Five
    b. Four
    c. Two
    d. Seven

> **Did you know?**
>
> Brad Bird's son voices the neighbor kid who is waiting for something amazing in the driveway.

316. When Mr. Incredible gets home and finds the message, what is the name that flashes on the screen as Mirage is talking?
    a. Freakazoid
    b. Trapezoid
    c. Omnidroid
    d. Teledroid

317. As Mr. Incredible looks around his office at the awards and mementos, which of these is *not* one of the names on the drawing of him saving a bus?
    a. Ginny
    b. Jamie
    c. Carrie
    d. Tilly

> **Did you know?**
>
> The phone number on the card that Mirage gives Mr. Incredible spells out SUPRHRO on the telephone keypad.

318. How does Mirage spy on Mr. Incredible while he battles the droid?
    a. Flower camera
    b. Bird camera
    c. Lava camera
    d. Coconut camera

319. What sits in the center of the table when Mr. Incredible has dinner with Mirage?
    a. A miniature volcano
    b. Flowers
    c. Salt and pepper
    d. Fruit

320. What does Mr. Incredible pull to work out?
    a. A train
    b. A car
    c. A building
    d. A bull

321. What is Mr. Incredibles waistline measurement after he has been working out?
    a. Fifty-six
    b. Forty-six
    c. Thirty-six
    d. Twenty-six

322. What does Edna tell her guard to check when Mr. Incredible arrives at her home?
    a. The piranha pool
    b. The attack dogs
    c. The trap door
    d. The electric fence

Did you know?

Edna Mode is a caricature of famed Hollywood designer Edith Head. Enda is voiced by none other than director Brad Bird.

323. What does Edna call Mr. Incredibles old superhero suit?
    a. Clown suit
    b. Hobo suit
    c. Vagabond suit
    d. Vagrant suit

324. As Edna is reminding Mr. Incredible about cape problems, how did Splash Down die?
    a. Stuck on a rocket
    b. Sucked into a jet engine
    c. Sucked into a vortex
    d. Snagged on takeoff

325. What does Mr. Incredible eat during his flight to the island?
    a. Shrimp cocktail
    b. A salad
    c. A steak
    d. Meatloaf

Did you know?

Mirage refers to room A113 for Mr. Incredibles briefing. This is a reference to Cal Arts classroom A113, where the animators went to school.

326. What piece of fruit does Mr. Incredible take when he arrives in his room on the island?
    a. Orange
    b. Apple
    c. Pear
    d. Grapes

327. As Edna demonstrated the new suits to Mrs. Incredible. What does Edna say Mrs. Incredibles suit breathes like?
    a. Silk
    b. Nylon
    c. Linen
    d. Egyptian cotton

328. What does Mr. Incredible throw at the guard as he sneaks into the secret lair on the island?
    a. Rock
    b. Coconut
    c. Palm tree
    d. Boulder

329. What is the figure called that Mr. Incredible picks up to attempt penetrating the lava wall?
    a. Winged Victory
    b. Moai
    c. Venus De Milo
    d. Hermes

330. Which of these is *not* one of the menu options after Mr. Incredible types the correct password?
    a. Evil plot
    b. Supers
    c. Finances
    d. Island operations

331. When Mr. Incredible finds the Project Kronos countdown, how much time is left on the display?
    a. 42 hours 8 minutes
    b. 10 hours 8 minutes
    c. 8 hours 10 minutes
    d. 42 hours 10 minutes

> **Did you know?**
>
> As Mrs. Incredible flies to the island, she radios India Golf Niner Niner; this references the movie The Iron Giant released in the year 1999.

332. As Mrs. Incredible talks to the babysitter, what does she say makes babies smarter?
    a. Mozart
    b. Beethoven
    c. Brahms
    d. Mendelssohn

333. After the family lands in the ocean, how does Mrs. Incredible know the family is about to be hit with debris?
    a. The kids tell her
    b. She looks up
    c. She senses it
    d. The reflection in the water

334. When Mr. Incredible threatens to crush Mirage, what does he compare her with?
    a. Broom
    b. Twig
    c. Toothpick
    d. Wooden spoon

335. When the family hides in the cave, what does Mrs. Incredible tell her children is their most valuable possession?
    a. Their identity
    b. Their family
    c. Their father
    d. Their superpowers

336. What does Mrs. Incredible tell violet is a luxury they cannot afford anymore?
    a. Fear
    b. Doubt
    c. Time
    d. Hesitating

Did you know?

As Mrs. Incredible spies on the control room, the energy level monitor is A1, and the chamber with the highest level is 13. This is another tribute to the A113 classroom at Cal Arts.

---

337. Who breaks Mr. Incredible out of the force field cell in the fortress?
    a. Mrs. Incredible
    b. Mirage
    c. Syndrome
    d. Dash

338. When Dash runs through the jungle away from the soldiers, what event trips him up?
    a. Bugs
    b. Booby trap
    c. Quicksand
    d. Surveillance plane

339. When the Incredible family is caught in the force fields, what does Mr. Incredible confess is his greatest adventure?
    a. His glory days
    b. His children
    c. His wife
    d. This adventure

340. How does Mirage suggest Mr. Incredible break into the computer?
    a. Hack the motherboard
    b. Punch the control panel
    c. She says the password is password
    d. Say please

341. What cologne does Frozone put on as the robot walks by his window?
    a. Brute
    b. Old Spice
    c. Drakar
    d. Hai Karate

342. When Frozone tells Honey that the city is in danger, what does she tell him is in danger?
    a. Her evening
    b. Their marriage
    c. His life
    d. The dinner

343. When the Incredibles arrive in the city, where does Mr. Incredible say they need to go?
    a. City hall
    b. Downtown
    c. The financial district
    d. The courthouse

Did you know?

As Mr. Incredible is fighting the robot, Doc Hudson from the movie *Cars* makes a cameo appearance on the street nearby.

344. As Mrs. Incredible sets the kids down on the side of the building, what sort of business is Lozano?
    a. Stockbrokers   c. Bank
    b. Record company   d. Publishing house

345. What does Mrs. Incredible use to take out the robot's gun?
    a. A newspaper   c. Sewer cover
       machine   d. A lamppost
    b. A car

Did you know?

The two elderly gentlemen who chat after the Incredibles stop the robot are a tribute to animators Frank Thomas and Ollie Johnston.

---

346. When the Incredibles lawyer rides with the family in the limousine, He tells them if Syndrome does what they will know?
    a. Sneeze   c. Move
    b. Invent   d. Shows his face

347. As Mrs. Incredible listens to the babysitter's phone messages, who is it that arrives as a replacement sitter?
    a. Honey   c. Mirage
    b. Edna   d. Syndrome

348. Which of these is *not* one of the superpowers Jack-Jack displays?
     a. Fire
     b. Invisibility
     c. Metal
     d. Evil baby

349. What is the name of the sports team that plays at Metroville Stadium?
     a. Spartans
     b. Broncos
     c. Vikings
     d. Super dudes

350. What does Violet offer to buy when Tony asks her on a date?
     a. Popcorn
     b. Soda
     c. Candy
     d. Ice cream

351. What is the name of the supervillain that comes from under the ground with a giant drill?
     a. The earthworm
     b. The mole
     c. The underminer
     d. The undertaker

Did you know?

This is the only Pixar film not to include the Pizza Planet truck or the Luxo ball.

Cars

352. On the inside of Lightning McQueen's rigs is a yellow sticker; what does this sticker read?
    a. Steel Ez
    b. Speed doctor
    c. Rust Ez
    d. Motion doctor

353. What is written on the side of the television camera filming the Piston Cup race?
    a. Peterson
    b. Nelson
    c. Smithson
    d. Thomson

354. What is written on the tire in the center of the track where the motorhomes are watching the race?
    a. Racing Zone
    b. Lightning Zone
    c. Redneck Hill
    d. Oil Can Hill

355. When the cars are in the pit area, what product does Leak Less advertised on the yellow car?
    a. Oil drums
    b. Adult drip pans
    c. Oil changing kits
    d. Leak sand

356. Which lap are the cars currently on after the major wreck on the track?
    a. 95
    b. 185
    c. 205
    d. 195

> *Did you know?*
>
> At lap 294, there is a brief glimpse of the #84 car with the Apple logo on the hood. Apple released its first computer.

357. When the press is interviewing lightning McQueen, what does he say he wanted to give the folks?
    a. Sizzle
    b. Excitement
    c. Pizzaz
    d. Sparkle

358. When the King approaches Lightning McQueen, he tells Lightning he has more talent in which part of his body?
    a. One windshield wiper
    b. One tail light
    c. One lug nut
    d. One turn signal

> *Did you know?*
>
> The King is voiced by racing royalty Richard Petty.

359. Which of these is *not* one of the magazines covers
     Lightning McQueen fantasizes about being on?
     - a. Rolling Tire
     - b. Vanity Plates
     - c. InDrive
     - d. Head and Tail
       Lights

360. When Lightning fantasizes about the movie he is
     featured in, what are the giant robots made from?
     - a. Gas cans
     - b. Mufflers
     - c. Spark plugs
     - d. Pistons

361. When Lightning is featured in the commercial for
     Rust Eze, how long will the results take according
     to the disclaimer?
     - a. Forty-six weeks
     - b. Thirty-six days
     - c. Thirty-six weeks
     - d. Fifty-six weeks

362. When Lightning enters the Rust Eze tent, and the
     spotlight hits him, what does a fan shout from the
     back?
     - a. Call Me the
       Breeze
     - b. Sweet Home
       Alabama
     - c. That Smell
     - d. Free bird

363. When Mack starts the trip to California, where does the East 64 exit take cars to?
    a. Truckville
    b. East Honkers
    c. Wingnut City
    d. Skid Mark Lane

Did you know?

As Mack is rolling down the road, there is a shot of the telephone wires with several small birds. This is a nod to the Pixar short *For the Birds*.

364. What is the name of the truck stop Mack tries to pull off the road into?
    a. Top Down
    b. Flaps up
    c. Headlights
    d. Eighteen Wheels

Did you know?

The number on the train Lightning McQueen is trying to cross ahead of is A113, the classroom at Cal Arts where the animators went to school.

365. When Lightning McQueen catches the truck that he thinks is Mack, what does this truck haul?
    a. Old tires
    b. Recycled batteries
    c. Cattle
    d. Rust Eze

366. When the statue of Stanley, the founder of Radiator Springs, shows, in which years was Radiator Springs founded?
    a. 1909
    b. 1919
    c. 1929
    d. 1905

367. Which of these is *not* one of the items advertised on Radiator Springs Curios?
    a. Bric-A-Brac
    b. Souvenirs
    c. Chachkies
    d. Trinkets

368. When the crew discovered Lightning McQueen is missing, which celebrity does the yellow Humvee imitate?
    a. Sylvester Stallone
    b. Arnold Schwarzenegger
    c. Dolph Lungren
    d. Chuck Norris

369. When Lightning wakes up at the impound, what does Mater call him?
    a. Rip Wan Winkle
    b. Snow White
    c. Rumpelstiltskin
    d. Sleeping Beauty

370. When Lightning McQueen enters the traffic courtroom, what does Ramone threaten to do to him?
    a. Rip his tires off
    b. Paint him pink
    c. Take a blow torch to him
    d. Drag him through a rock bed

371. Where does Lightning McQueen say his lawyer is when he is in the courtroom?
    a. Los Angeles
    c. Hawaii
    b. Barbados
    d. Tahiti

372. Above the courtroom door are the Latin words "Justitae Via Strat Veritate" what does this translate to in English?
    a. The way of justice is paved with truth
    c. The way of justice is the body
    b. The way of justice is by force
    d. The way of justice is written in Latin

373. How much does Mater say Lightning McQueen owes him in legal fees?
    a. Thirty-two dollars
    c. Thirty thousand dollars
    b. Thirty-two thousand dollars
    d. Thirteen thousand dollars

Did you know?

As Lightning McQueen tries to escape from Radiator Springs, all of the rock formations are in the shape of car parts.

Did you know?

Luigi's license plate is the coordinates for the Ferrari factory in Italy.

374. What are the flowers from the fire truck waters outside Luigi's made of?
    a. Sparks plugs
    b. Headlights
    c. Hubcaps
    d. Taillights

375. When Sally tries to get the tourists to stay at the Cozy Cone Motel, what does she offer for free?
    a. Road maps
    b. Lincoln continental breakfast
    c. Postcards
    d. Air fresheners

376. What does the bumper sticker read that Lizzie slaps on the tourist bumper?
    a. Radiator Springs
    b. Filler up
    c. Nice Butte
    d. Ornament Valley

377. When Doc Hudson challenges Lightning McQueen to a race, finish this line by Lightning, "Float like a Cadillac, sting like a _____."
    a. Buick
    b. Bentley
    c. BMW
    d. Beemer

378. When Fillmore offers Lightning organic fuel, what does Sarge call his fuel?
    a. Freak juice
    b. High octane
    c. Flying fuel
    d. Tickle juice

379. What does Lightning McQueen notice on Sally that she is embarrassed about?
    a. Custom license plate
    b. Pinstripe tattoo
    c. Customer bumper
    d. Cars rock group bumper sticker

380. When Mater takes Lightning McQueen tractor tipping, what vehicle is Frank?
    a. Harrower
    b. Cement mixer
    c. Baler
    d. Harvester

381. What is Sally's nickname for Lightning McQueen?
    a. Headlights
    b. Wheels
    c. Stickers
    d. Speedy

382. When Sarge raises the American flag, what does Fillmore have playing next door?
    a. *The National Anthem*
    b. *America the Beautiful*
    c. *God Bless America*
    d. *Living in America*

> *Did you know?*
>
> When Doc Hudson examines the Sheriff, there is an X-ray of an engine on the lightbox.

383. Which of these is *not* one of the years Doc Hudson won the Piston Cup?
    - a. 1952
    - b. 1951
    - c. 1955
    - d. 1953

384. Which car does Flo say is for her husband?
    - a. Sherriff
    - b. Ramone
    - c. Luigi
    - d. Fillmore

385. When Sally shows Lightning the Wheel Well Motel, what are the bugs flying around the pump made from?
    - a. Dodge Dart
    - b. AMC Gremlin
    - c. VW Beetles
    - d. Piaggio Vespa

386. What does Mater tell Lightning McQueen their alibi was for tractor tipping?
    - a. Comparting stickers
    - b. Shooting old tires
    - c. Playing brake shoes
    - d. Smashing mailboxes

387. Which car stops the tractor stampede through the middle of town?
    - a. Mater
    - b. Sherriff
    - c. Fire engine
    - d. Doc Hudson

388. What incident ended Doc Hudson's racing career?
     a. Crash
     b. Got too old
     c. Tire blow out
     d. Scandal

389. What is the name of the white wall tires Luigi insists Lightning McQueen purchase?
     a. Mussolini
     b. Fettuccini Alfredo
     c. Tread Stars
     d. Wire walls

390. What does the sign on the gun Sarge show Lightning McQueen read?
     a. Guaranteed no misses
     b. Guaranteed no hitchhikers
     c. Guaranteed no speeders
     d. Guaranteed no tailgaters

391. Finish the pumper stick that reads, "You tailgate, I _____."
     a. Slow down
     b. Stop
     c. Backfire
     d. Honk

392. Which of these is *not* one of the bumper stickers Lizzie puts on Lightning McQueen's bumper?
     a. Scottsdale
     b. Kingman
     c. Barstow
     d. San Bernardino

393. Who tipped the press off that Lightning McQueen was in Radiator Springs?
     a. Mater
     b. Sally
     c. Doc Hudson
     d. Sherriff

> *Did you know?*
>
> When the cars are outside the Los Angeles International Speedway, the Pizza Planet truck is in the crowd next to the Elvis Presley car.

> *Did you know?*
>
> As the commentator reports that everything is shut down for the race, the city sign for Emeryville is shown, Emeryville is the home base for Pixar.

394. When Doc Hudson shows up at the race, how many years has it been since he has been seen?
    a. Fifty   c. Thirty
    b. Forty   d. Twenty

> *Did you know?*
>
> When Lightning McQueen starts driving backward, you can hear Mater say, "Git 'R Done." Larry, the Cable guy, made this phrase popular, and this actor voices Mater.

395. When Mater gets his ride in the helicopter, what does he say he is as happy as?
    a. Dog in a forest
    b. Tornado in a trailer park
    c. Bee smothered in honey
    d. Kitten in a tree

Did you know?

During the credits, the same car carrying the mattress can be seen leaving Luigi's.

396. When Mater give the tour of the museum, how many wins did Doc Hudson have in 1952?
    a. Seventy-two
    b. Three
    c. Twenty-seven
    d. Eight-three

397. What movie is playing at the Radiator Springs drive-in theater?
    a. Toy Car Story
    b. Gone with the Wingnut
    c. Finding Nissan
    d. Monster Trucks

Did you know?

The voice artists from *Toy Story*, *Monster's Inc.*, and *A Bug's Life* come back to do the voices for the cars in the various movies at the drive-in.

Ratatouille

398. How long in advance is Gusteau's restaurant booked for reservations?
    a. Seven months
    b. Six months
    c. Five months
    d. Five years

399. Which of these is *not* one of the magazine covers of Gusteau shown on the television?
    a. Bon Appetite
    b. Gourmet
    c. Food & Wine
    d. French Fare

400. What is Anton Ego's restaurant column titled?
    a. The Fancy Feast
    b. The Grim Eater
    c. The Elegant Eater
    d. The Final Review

401. What is Remy's job in the rat pack?
    a. Lookout
    b. Food finder
    c. Poison checker
    d. Chef

402. What does Remy use as a plate when he eats garbage with his family?
    a. Bottlecap
    b. Button
    c. Piece of cardboard
    d. A broken piece of plate

403. When Remy is watching the television with Gusteau's show, what does Gusteau compare good food with?
    a. Painting
    b. Music
    c. Dancing
    d. Sculpting

404. What does Remy use as a rotisserie to cook his mushroom on the chimney?
    a. Wire hanger
    b. Telephone wire
    c. Stick
    d. TV Antenna

405. What item sits on the same shelf as the television in the elderly woman's home?
    a. Picture frame
    b. Vase
    c. Telephone
    d. Fan

406. Where does the elderly woman store the shotgun she grabs to get rid of Remy and Emile?
    a. Umbrella stand
    b. Closet
    c. Refrigerator
    d. Next to her chair

407. What do the rats give Remy to grab onto when they are floating down the river?
    a. Spatula
    b. Spoon
    c. Fork
    d. Knife

Did you know?

The dog that barks at Remy when he explores the various apartments has the same silhouette as Dug from the film *Up!*.

408. What is the young woman doing that Remy sees in the round window as he continues his exploration?
     a. Getting dressed
     b. Brushing her hair
     c. Putting on lipstick
     d. Putting on shoes

409. What is the name of Linguini's mother?
     a. Ralline
     b. Rene
     c. Renata
     d. Rochelle

410. When Remy takes a ride on the serving cart from the kitchen, what is the waiter reaching for when he grabs Remy?
     a. Teacup
     b. Peppermill
     c. Serving utensil
     d. Napkins

411. What does Linguini hide Remy underneath when the chef comes looking for the soup?
     a. Colander
     b. Pan
     c. Mop bucket
     d. Ladle

412. When the chef tries to stop the soup from leaving the kitchen, what is in the box he runs into?
     a. Tomatoes
     b. Carrots
     c. Onions
     d. Potatoes

413. When Linguini is watching television in his apart-
     ment, what channel is he watching?
     a. Eight
     b. Twelve
     c. Three
     d. Two

414. What does Remy use as a bed when staying with
     Linguini?
     a. Sock
     b. Kitchen towel
     c. Throw pillow
     d. Oven mitt

415. What time is on the clock when Remy and Linguini
     have omelets together?
     a. 8:07
     b. 1:35
     c. 7:08
     d. 8:14

Did you know?

When Linguini and Remy are outside the restaurant,
Linguini is trying to find a place to smuggle Remy into
the building. When he opens the front of his pants, he
is wearing Incredibles underwear.

416. When Linguini gives Remy a piece of cheese in the
     refrigerator, what sits on the tray with Remy?
     a. Asparagus
     b. Mushrooms
     c. Sausage
     d. Caviar

Did you know?

The brand of spaghetti Linguini places on the counter is
Bouchiba. This is a nod to animator Bolhem Bouchiba.

> *Did you know?*
>
> The label on the bottle of wine he pours himself is Lasseter Cabernet, a nod to producer/director John Lasseter.

417. What is the statute of limitation on Gusteau's will to find an heir?
   a. Two years   c. Two months
   b. One year   d. Twenty years

418. There is an award sitting next to the case where Gusteau's hat is on display. What shape is this award?
   a. Chef's hat   c. Spoon
   b. Spatula   d. Whisk

419. Just above the five stars plaque on the wall in Gusteau's office, there is a large gold plaque in the shape of what item?
   a. Spatula   c. Meat cleaver
   b. Peppermill   d. Toothpick

> *Did you know?*
>
> As Collette works with Linguini, there is a small burn on the inside of her wrist. This small detail is significant since most chefs have a similar burn while working in a kitchen.

420. Collette shares information about the chefs with Linguini; how old was Lalo when he ran away from home to join the circus?
    a. Thirteen
    c. Fourteen
    b. Twelve
    d. Eight

421. As Horst shares why he has gone to jail, which of these is *not* one of the stories he tells why he was arrested?
    a. Robbed the second largest bank in France
    c. Stole the prime minister of France ballpoint pen
    b. Defraud a major corporation
    d. Killed a man with his thumb

422. The Sweetbread recipe the chef recommends to Linguini for the customers contains anchovy sauce with what other ingredient?
    a. Licorice
    c. Brandy
    b. Buttermilk
    d. Squid ink

> **Did you know?**
>
> The 1961 Chateau Latour chef serves Linguini in his office and is currently priced at $5,000.00 per bottle.

423. When Remy and Emile find each other in the alley, what does Emile say he thinks he is eating?
    a. Old sausage
    c. Part of a paper plate
    b. An old shoe
    d. Some sort of wrapper

424. During the party the rats throw for Remy; what do the rat drummer use as drumsticks?
    - a. Chopsticks
    - b. Toothpicks
    - c. Matchsticks
    - d. Pencils

425. When Remy's dad is talking to him about looking thin, what does he say he has a surplus of?
    - a. Attitude
    - b. Snobbery
    - c. Haughtiness
    - d. Bragging

426. What does Remy use as a cup while talking with his dad?
    - a. Bottlecap
    - b. Acorn shell
    - c. Toothpaste cap
    - d. Dollhouse bowl

427. What is the bicyclist carrying in his basket when he crashes into the blue car after seeing Remy on the street?
    - a. Fruit
    - b. Wine
    - c. Flowers
    - d. Baguettes

Did you know?

Collette drives a Calahan motorcycle. This is a nod to Sharon Calahan, director of photography.

428. When Linguini is trying to tell Collette about Remy, what object does she pull out of her purse to protect herself as he rambles?
    - a. Pepper spray
    - b. A pen
    - c. Her keys
    - d. Hair spray

> **Did you know?**
>
> The typewriter used by Anton Ego has the appearance of a skull from behind. His office resembles a coffin when viewed from above.

429. When Anton Ego tries to guess what the news is about Gusteau's, what new microwavable dish does he guess Gusteau's is releasing?
    - a. Beef Wellington
    - b. Beef Bourguignon
    - c. Eggrolls
    - d. Chop Suey

430. Which famous chef does Anton Ego compare Chef Gusteau with?
    - a. Hamburger helper
    - b. Chef Boyardee
    - c. Top Ramen
    - d. McDonald's

431. Which of these is *not* one of the current Gusteau's frozen food posters in the Chef's office?
    - a. Hamburgers
    - b. Tooth Pickin' Chicken
    - c. Haggis
    - d. Burritos

> **Did you know?**
>
> The Pizza Planet truck appears on the bridge when the chef is chasing Remy through Paris.

432. When chef Skinner chases Remy through Paris to retrieve the letter, Remy jumps aboard a boat with the words "Defense De Fumer" painted on the deck. What does this translate to in English?
    a. No life vests
    b. No spitting
    c. No running
    d. No smoking

433. Linguini's picture appears on the front page of Le Journal. What article is featured on page 19 of this newspaper?
    a. Out on the town
    b. Create a memorable menu
    c. A perfect day for a perfect Souffle
    d. A fresh surprise from an old master

434. When the hef Skinner reads the newspaper about Linguini, where does the paper say Ego is visiting?
    a. Dijon
    b. Giverny
    c. Champagne
    d. Bordeaux

Did you know?

While Linguini and Collette are skating on the bridge near Notre Dame, the villain Bomb Voyage from *The Incredibles* performs for the tourists in the background.

435. What is the first opening the health inspector has on his calendar when the Chef calls him about a rat infestation?
    a. Six months
    b. Three months
    c. Three years
    d. Three days

436. What does Emile hide inside when Linguini comes back to the restaurant to find Remy?
    a. Asparagus
    b. Grapes
    c. In the black tiles
    d. In a box

437. When Linguini is dreaming, what does Anton Ego tell Linguini he wants when he arrives to take Ego's order?
    a. His brain lightly sauteed in garlic
    b. His tongue boiled to perfection
    c. His heart roasted on a spit
    d. His spleen broiled with potatoes

438. What does Emile drop on the trunk of Skinner's car to free Remy?
    a. Traffic light
    b. Gargoyle
    c. Flowerpot
    d. Tree

439. What does team five handle when Remy's rat friends help him cook?
    a. Sauces
    b. Roasted items
    c. Fish
    d. Grill

440. What does Linguini use to help him serve the restaurant while the rats cook?
    a. Skateboard
    b. Scooter
    c. Roller skates
    d. Hoverboard

441. As Anton Ego tries the Ratatouille, he has a flashback to his childhood. What is sitting on the grass behind him when he stands at the door?
    a. A bicycle
    b. A dog
    c. A ball
    d. A chicken

442. What type of ball is sitting beneath the chair on Ego's home as he stands in the doorway?
    a. Basketball
    b. Baseball
    c. Soccer ball
    d. Softball

443. What is the citation code on the health department sign that is displayed on Gusteau's restaurant?
    a. A113
    b. 114030
    c. 403011
    d. 301140

444. What does the rat hold in his paws on the La Ratatouille sign outside Linguini's bistro?
    a. Bottle of wine
    b. Whisk
    c. Fork
    d. Spoon

WALL-E

445. What famous musical is the song *Put on Your Sunday Clothes* from?
    a. *Easter Parade*
    b. *Oklahoma!*
    c. *Calamity Jane*
    d. *Hello Dolly*

446. When WALL-E runs over the newspaper, what does the logo on the front of the podium read in the photograph?
    a. United States on BNL
    b. Global CEO
    c. BNL CEO
    d. BNL countries

Did you know?

WALL-E's cockroach friend is called HAL. This is a reference to HAL 9000 from the film *2001 A Space Odyssey*.

447. According to the advertisements, how many years were the people of earth supposed to spend on the Axiom?
    a. Ten years
    b. Twenty years
    c. Five years
    d. Thirty years

> *Did you know?*
>
> Rex from *Toy Story* can be seen behind the two bowling pins in WALL-E's house.

448. Where does WALL-E store his videotape while he is at work?
    a. Cooler
    b. Refrigerator
    c. Shelf
    d. Toaster

> *Did you know?*
>
> WALL-E has Mr. Fredrickson's cane complete with tennis balls standing upside down next to his monitor in his house.

> *Did you know?*
>
> EVE was designed and created by Pixar with assistance by the developers at Apple.

449. As EVE searches the Buy N Large, what sort of sale does the banner read about her?
    - a. Clean up sale
    - b. End of earth sale
    - c. Evacuation sale
    - d. Axiom sale

450. What sort of children's toy does EVE scan as she searches the Buy N Large?
    - a. Pinwheel
    - b. Yo-Yo
    - c. Hula hoop
    - d. Rubik's Cube

Did you know?

The statue of EVE that WALL-E builds includes the Luxo lamp.

451. What does WALL-E use for eyes on the statue of EVE he builds?
    - a. Christmas lights
    - b. Sapphires
    - c. Headlights
    - d. Christmas ornaments

Did you know?

Eve scans the wreckage of the Pizza Planet truck as she searches the city.

452. What is EVE's response when WALL-E asks for her directive?
    - a. Classified
    - b. Plant
    - c. Top Secret
    - d. Search mission

453. When WALL-E takes EVE home, what song does the animated fish sing?
    a. *It's a Small World*
    b. *Don't Worry, Be Happy*
    c. *Fishin' In the Dark*
    d. *California Girls*

454. What kitchen appliance does EVE break while experimenting with it?
    a. Toaster
    b. Can opener
    c. Potato peeler
    d. Hand mixer

455. What children's toy does EVE solve within seconds in WALL-E house?
    a. Rubik's Cube
    b. Jigsaw puzzle
    c. Word search
    d. Crossword puzzle

456. What item in WALL-E's collection does EVE show him what its purpose really is?
    a. Fork
    b. Drum
    c. Candle
    d. Lighter

457. After EVE takes the plant and powers down, what object does WALL-E use to pry open her battery compartment?
    a. Crowbar
    b. Hammer
    c. Screwdriver
    d. His hands

458. What does WALL-E use as a boat to take EVE down the sewer?
    a. A rubber raft
    b. Another WALL-E
    c. Corrugated sheet metal
    d. An old tire

459. What video game does WALL-E play on the Atari game console?
    a. Tennis
    b. Pong
    c. Tetris
    d. Breakout

Did you know?

As WALL-E rides outside the rocket going to space, the SPUTNIK satellite gets caught on his face. SPUTNIK is the first satellite to be placed in orbit.

Did you know?

When WALL-E arrives on the Axiom, he is on Deck A 224; this is another reference to A113, with the number one-off. A113 is the classroom at Cal Arts where the animators attended school.

460. When WALL-E tries to catch up with EVE, he runs into a human in a hoverchair. What does the human suggest doing today?
   a. Play virtual tennis
   b. Hit virtual baseballs
   c. Play virtual football
   d. Hit virtual golf balls

461. What is the temperature on the Axiom according to the BNL virtual sun?
   a. 82 degrees
   b. 72 degrees
   c. 27 degrees
   d. 32 degrees

462. What is the name of the man WALL-E helps back into his chair?
   a. John
   b. Greg
   c. Tom
   d. Bob

Did you know?

The carpet on the daycare center floor is the same pattern as the wallpaper in Andy's room in *Toy Story 2*.

463. According to the advertisement, what is the new red?
   a. Yellow
   b. Pink
   c. Green
   d. Blue

464. What feature does Mary say she did not realize they had on the Axiom?
   a. A pool
   b. A movie theater
   c. A beauty salon
   d. A restaurant

> *Did you know?*
>
> The navigators' display flashes A113 when it discovers EVE has come back with the plant. This is another reference to the Cal Arts classroom.

465. When WALL-E falls through to the captain's quarters, a display of the Axioms captains is on the wall. Which captain was in charge from 2248 – 2379?
    a. Captain Reardon
    b. Captain Fee
    c. Captain Thompson
    d. Captain Brace

466. When the captain reaches the bridge, what song is playing in the background?
    a. *Sleeping Beauty Waltz*
    b. *The Minuet Waltz*
    c. *Gartenlaube Waltz*
    d. *The Blue Danube*

> *Did you know?*
>
> Oscar-nominated actress Sigourney Weaver is the voice of the bridge on the Axiom.

467. What do the passengers of the Axiom get in celebration of the Septuacentennial anniversary?
    a. Steak in a cup
    b. Cupcake in a cup
    c. Ice cream sundae
    d. Champagne cocktail

468. When the captain pushes the green button on the bridge and the video starts, what does the global CEO say they can start?
    a. Operation cleanup
    b. Operation replant
    c. Operation recolonization
    d. Operation Earth

469. When the captain sends EVE to the repair ward, what does he tell the navigator to do to WALL-E?
    a. Get serviced
    b. Get cleaned
    c. Sent back to Earth
    d. Advise the crew

470. What does the announcement system call the robots when EVE takes back her arms from WALL-E?
    a. Rogue
    b. Dangerous
    c. Defective
    d. Lethal

471. What is the robot doing when WALL-E and EVE arrive back on the ship?
    a. Changing lightbulbs
    b. Cleaning
    c. Monitoring the weather
    d. Welding

472. How does WALL-E travel from the Lido deck to the captain's bridge?
    a. The outside of the ship
    b. The maintenance corridor
    c. The elevator
    d. The garbage chute

473. In which year was the message to override the return to Earth given to the autopilots?
   a. 2113
   b. 2110
   c. 2022
   d. 2235

> *Did you know?*
>
> The mice that are crawling on EVE when she is sent to the garbage area were computer mice. They are called REM-E, named for the character Remy from the Pixar film *Ratatouille*.

474. When EVE is trying to take the plant to the bridge with WALL-E, they encounter a wall of security robots. Which of the malfunctioning robots stop the security robots for them?
   a. Massage robot
   b. Vacuum robot
   c. Tennis robot
   d. Beauty robot

475. What event brings WALL-E's memory back after EVE repairs him on Earth?
   a. Seeing HAL
   b. Holding EVE's hand
   c. Hearing his favorite song
   d. Seeing his things

> *Did you know?*
>
> During the credits, there is a picture of four pods with the people in the center. WALL-E can be seen in the upper right corner. The cogs of WALL-E's feet make a hidden Mickey.

Did you know?

The mosaic of the sea creatures includes Crush and Squirt from *Finding Nemo*.

UP

476. What is the name of the newsreel that creates Spotlight on Adventure?
    a. Hollywoodland
    c. Movietown
    b. Reeltown
    d. Toontown

477. What is the vehicle that Charles Muntz uses to travel to Paradise Falls called?
    a. Airship
    c. Gondola
    b. Balloon
    d. Dirigible

478. What does Elie use to pretend she is Charles Muntz?
    a. An old car
    c. A cardboard box
    b. An old house
    d. A treehouse

479. When Carl finds Elie playing, he reads the newspaper clippings on the wall. How high did Muntz climb to break the altitude record?
    a. 47,973
    c. 43,976
    b. 49,376
    d. 46,379

Did you know?

Pete Docter's daughter Elie is the inspiration for the character of Elie. Docter even used her as the voice actress for the role.

480. What does Elie use as a badge for the Explorer's Club?
    a. Bottlecap
    b. Button
    c. Coin
    d. Milk lid

481. What does Elie attach Carl's balloon to when she send it to him through his window?
    a. Her arm
    b. Candy bar
    c. Rock
    d. Stick

482. Where did Elie get the picture of Paradise Falls she has in her adventure book?
    a. A magazine
    b. A library book
    c. An encyclopedia
    d. A newspaper

483. What objects sit on the blanket next to Elie as she and Carl look up at the clouds?
    a. Bottle of wine
    b. Loaf of bread
    c. Camera
    d. Wheel of cheese

484. What color is the kerchief Elie wears when she and Carl work at the zoo?
    a. Blue
    b. Pink
    c. Green
    d. Orange

485. What adorns the mobile Carl and Elie hang above the crib in the nursery?
    a. Blimps
    b. Birds
    c. Balloons
    d. Clouds

486. Which of these is *not* one of the things Carl and Elie spend their Paradise Falls money on?
    a. House flood
    b. Fix the roof
    c. Flat tire
    d. Broken leg

Did you know?

The brochure on the travel agent's desk has a scene from the Pixar short Knick Knack on the front.

487. What is written on the box of breakfast cereal Carl has sitting on the kitchen table after Elie passes away?
    a. Shredded Wheat
    b. Flakes
    c. Fruit O's
    d. Bran

488. What is the name of the retirement village on the pamphlet Carl gets in the mail?
    a. Shady Acres
    b. Shady Oaks
    c. Twilight Years
    d. Golden Acres

489. What business stands across the street from Carl's house when he is talking with the construction worker?
    a. Donut shop
    b. Convenience store
    c. Sushi
    d. Pets store

490. What did Carl pour in the gas tank of the construction boss?
    a. Sugar
    b. Prune juice
    c. Cream
    d. Tomato juice

491. Which Wilderness Explorer troupe is Russell a part of?
    a. Thirty-two
    b. Forty-five
    c. Twenty-four
    d. Fifty-four

492. What does Carl tell Russell the snipe gobbles up in his yard?
    a. Azaleas
    b. Petunias
    c. Daisies
    d. Tulips

Did you know?

The courtroom Carl is sitting outside of is A113. This is a reference to the Cal Arts classroom where the Pixar animators went to school.

Did you know?

The animators at Pixar confirmed that there were 20,622 balloons animated in the lift-off of the house scene. Later, when the house is seen flying, there are 10.297 balloons animated.

> **Did you know?**
>
> You can see the Luxo ball and Lots-O'-Huggin' Bear on the floor in the room the child is playing in when the house flats by.

493. Which of these is *not* one of the colors of the flowers on the wall of the child's bedroom the house floats by?
     a. Green
     b. Pink
     c. Blue
     d. Orange

> **Did you know?**
>
> The Pizza Planet truck is parked on the street as Carl's house floats through the city.

494. What object is featured on the billboard on the top of the building Carl's house floats by?
     a. Car
     b. Airplane
     c. Boat
     d. Train

495. What kitchen appliance does Carl use to maneuver the weather vane on the roof of the house?
     a. Blender
     b. Coffee grinder
     c. Toaster
     d. Oven

496. What type of clouds does Russell identify as the clouds they are heading into?
     a. Cirrocumulus
     b. Nimbostratus
     c. Cumulonimbus
     d. Stratocumulus

497. Who gave Russell his Wilderness Explorer GPS?
    a. His dad
    b. His Mom
    c. His grandfather
    d. His uncle

498. How many transfers does Russell say it will take for him to get home on the bus from South America?
    a. A bzillion
    b. A million
    c. A thousand
    d. A billion

499. What does Carl grab onto to keep his house from floating away when he falls out?
    a. Water pipe
    b. Balloon strings
    c. Garden hose
    d. Electrical wire

500. When Russell suggests they walk the house over to the falls from where they are, what does he compare the floating house to?
    a. Parade balloon
    b. Kite
    c. Giant dog
    d. Glider

501. How long do Carl and Russell have to get the house over to the falls before the balloons deflate?
    a. One week
    b. Two days
    c. Three weeks
    d. Three days

502. What interferes with the dogs as they chase the bird through the jungle?
    a. The floating house
    b. Carl's hearing aid
    c. Carl and Russel
    d. Another animal

503. When Russell starts complaining about being too tired to walk anymore, what does Carl tell him will eat him?
    a. Tigers
    b. Lions
    c. Alligators
    d. Hippopotamus

Did you know?

One of the badges on Russell's uniform is the Luxo ball.

---

504. What does Russell name the bird he finds in the jungle?
    a. Carl
    b. Kevin
    c. Mr. Frederickson
    d. Elie

505. What color of the balloon does Kevin eat when he gets on the roof of the house?
    a. Blue
    b. Yellow
    c. Green
    d. Pink

506. When Carl hears someone speaking to them, what does he mistake for a human?
    a. Rocks
    b. Bushes
    c. An animal
    d. Clouds

507. When Russell gives the command to speak, what are the first words the dog says to them?
    a. I love you
    b. Hi there
    c. My name is Dug
    d. Bark bark

508. Which of these is *not* one of the scents the dog pack picks up when they find the bird print in the dirt?
   a. Chocolate
   b. Denture cream
   c. Prunes
   d. Bengay

509. What breed of dog is Alpha, the leader of the dog pack?
   a. Rottweiler
   b. Doberman pinscher
   c. Golden retriever
   d. Bulldog

510. What does Carl call Dug and Kevin when he tells Russell not to wake them up?
   a. Traveling goof patrol
   b. Traveling clown troop
   c. Traveling flea circus
   d. Traveling zoo

511. What animal does Carl hit, thinking it is his alarm clock the next morning?
   a. Frog
   b. Bird
   c. Squirrel
   d. Grasshopper

512. What does Alpha call Russell when they track them down to find Kevin?
   a. Small person
   b. Small soldier
   c. Small policeman
   d. Small mailman

513. When the dogs surround Carl and Russell, what does Charles Muntz say to stop the dogs from attacking?
   a. Sit
   b. Heel
   c. Stay
   d. Halt

514. Which of these is *not* one of the cities Charles Muntz refers to when he talks about where his collection is housed?
    a. Munich
    b. Paris
    c. New York
    d. London

515. Which President was Charles on safari with when he found the giant Somalian leopard tortoise?
    a. Coolidge
    b. Truman
    c. Hoover
    d. Roosevelt

> *Did you know?*
>
> The spots on the giant Somalian leopard tortoise make a hidden Mickey.

516. What card game did Charles Muntz play with the president while on safari?
    a. Gin rummy
    b. Poker
    c. Bridge
    d. Cribbage

517. What dessert offering does Charles Muntz tell Carl and Russell Epsilon makes?
    a. Bananas foster
    b. Cherries jubilee
    c. Apple brown betty
    d. Peach cobbler

518. What does Russell give to Carl when they finally bring the house to Paradise Falls?
    a. His badges
    b. His backpack
    c. His hat
    d. His GPS

519. After Carl pastes Paradise Falls' picture into the adventure book, he turns the page and finds a drawing of what animal on the next page?
    a. Penguin   c. Jaguar
    b. Platypus   d. Armadillo

520. When Russell straps the balloons to his back to help Kevin, what does he use to propel himself through the air?
    a. An umbrella   c. He blows on the
    b. A fan   balloons
                              d. Leaf blower

521. Which of these is the last item Carl throws out of the house to make it light enough to float once more?
    a. Refrigerator   c. Kitchen table
    b. Paradise falls jar   d. A box of pictures

522. When Dug knocks on the door of the house, why does he tell Carl he was hiding under the porch?
    a. He was afraid   c. He loves him
    b. He was lonesome   d. He wants to help

Did you know?

As Russell catches up with the dirigible, the dogs are playing poker. This is a reference to the paintings by artist Cassius Marcellus Coolidge in 1894.

523. What are the dogs using for chips when they are playing poker?
    a. Dog bones
    b. Kibble
    c. Crackers
    d. Money

524. What does Charles Muntz call the head dog when he orders them to take down the house?
    a. Red leader
    b. Gray leader
    c. Blue leader
    d. Black leader

525. What does Carl defense himself with when Charles Muntz attacks him with a sword?
    a. A hammer
    b. A dog toy
    c. A fossil
    d. His cane

526. How does Russell stop the dogs from attacking the house?
    a. He throws a bone
    b. He yells squirrel
    c. He takes down their planes
    d. He throws a ball

Did you know?

Director Pete Docter is the voice of the troop leader at the badge ceremony.

527. What does Jimmy get his badge for at the Wilderness Explorer ceremony?
   a. Wild animal defensive arts
   b. Extreme mountaineering lore
   c. Assisting the elderly
   d. Creative gardening

Did you know?

In Oakland, California, Fenton's Ice Cream, where Carl takes Russell after the Wilderness Explorer ceremony, is actually an ice cream shop.

---

528. During the credits, where does Carl take Russell on the Executive Producer page of the adventure book?
   a. Camping museum
   b. Zoo
   c. The forest
   d. Fishing

529. What instrument does Carl play on the "Music By" page of the adventure book?
   a. Kazoo
   b. Water glasses
   c. Trumpet
   d. Accordion

530. What movie did Carl take Russell to see on the "Film Editor" page of the adventure book?
   a. The Avengers
   b. Cars
   c. Star Wars
   d. Jaws

Toy Story III

531. What does Mrs. Potato Head hold in her hand opposite her handbag when she attacks Woody on top of the train?
    - a. Gun
    - b. Whip
    - c. Bat
    - d. Nunchuks

532. What toy plays the part of the orphans on the train during playtime?
    - a. Little people
    - b. Troll dolls
    - c. Green army men
    - d. Barbie dolls

Did you know?

The engine number 95 is a reference to 1995, the year the first *Toy Story* film was released.

533. What object sits at the bottom of the Border Crossing sign in the desert?
    - a. Rock
    - b. Cactus
    - c. Cattle skull
    - d. Lasso

534. What is written on the button evil Dr. Porkchop presses to finish Buzz, Woody, and Jessie?
    a. Death by monkeys
    b. Death by aliens
    c. Death by water
    d. Death by fire

535. When Andy measures his toy's height on the door frame, what does the shortest marker say?
    a. Slinky
    b. Hamm
    c. Slinky's butt
    d. Potato head

536. While Andy is watching the movie with his toys, which toy does he give a piece of popcorn to?
    a. Rex
    b. Bo peep
    c. Wheezy
    d. Woody

537. What animal appears on the poster on the back of Andy's bedroom door?
    a. Shark
    b. Dinosaur
    c. Dog
    d. Tiger

538. What is the total of the book Woody stands on for the staff meeting after Andy leaves the bedroom?
    a. Thesaurus
    b. Economics
    c. Government
    d. Super encyclopedia

539. When Buzz tells the toys they are going to attic mode, what does he tell them to keep with them at all times?
    a. Wits about them
    b. Their moving buddy
    c. Their accessories
    d. Hopes up

540. As the green army men go AWOL, they tell the other toys they are the first to go when what object comes out?
    a. Trash bag
    b. Cardboard box
    c. Moving van
    d. Storage container

Did you know?

The racecar poster on Andy's wall is Finn McMissle from Cars 2. There is also a pennant with P.U. on the wall. This is a nod to Pixar University, a real education program.

Did you know?

When Woody looks at the bulletin board in Andy's room, there is a letter from State University in Emeryville, CA. This is the town where the headquarters of Pixar is located.

541. According to the ticket stub on his bulletin board, what band did Andy go to see at Tri-County Arena on November 17?
    a. Carl and the Frederickson's
    b. Nemoria
    c. Humble Beginnings
    d. The Tigers

Did you know?

The world map on Andy's wall has several push pins at various places around the United States. These pins represent the home towns of the Pixar animators.

542. What is the name of the magazine Molly is reading when she starts sorting through her toys?
    a. Half Beat
    b. Tween
    c. High School Musical
    d. Teen Beauty

543. Which toy says they get the corvette after they see Mollie place Barbie in the Sunnyside box?
    a. Jessie
    b. Mr. Potato Head
    c. Buzz
    d. Hamm

Did you know?

The garbageman is wearing the same shirt Sid wears in the first *Toy Story* film. It has been confirmed that this is Sid from the first *Toy Story* film.

> *Did you know?*
>
> Andy's mom's car's license plate is A113, the classroom at Cal Arts where the Pixar animators went to school.

544. What toy is Bonnie playing with when Andy's mom arrives at the daycare center with the toys?
    a. Ken doll
    b. Lotso
    c. Big baby
    d. Mechanical monkey

545. Which toy is the first to welcome the new toys to the Butterfly room?
    a. Purple octopus
    b. Jack in the box
    c. Lotso
    d. Crocodile

546. What song is playing when Ken first sees Barbie at the daycare center?
    a. *Dream Weaver*
    b. *Dream On*
    c. *Stayin' Alive*
    d. *Night Fever*

> *Did you know?*
>
> After the introductions are finished, as the toys walk away, you can see two toys in the background that resemble Sulley and Boo from *Monsters Inc.*

547. When Ken begs Barbie to come to live in his dream house, who does he compare himself to?
     a. Luke Skywalker
     b. The Six Million Dollar Man
     c. GI Joe
     d. Evil Kinevil

548. As the janitor cleans the restroom at the daycare center, what is written on his shirt?
     a. Mr. Tony
     b. Mr. Walt
     c. Mr. Steve
     d. Mr. John

549. When the daycare supervisor finds Bonnie playing on the playground, what children's game is Bonnie playing?
     a. Hula hoop
     b. Jump rope
     c. Jacks
     d. Hopscotch

550. When Woody climbs on the roof to escape the daycare center, he looks out over the playground. What sort of flowers are painted along the walls of the playground?
     a. Daisies
     b. Sunflowers
     c. Tulips
     d. Snapdragons

551. What item does Woody find on the daycare center's roof to help aid him in his escape?
     a. Frisbee
     b. Parachute
     c. Kite
     d. Pogo stick

> *Did you know?*
>
> As Woody hangs from the tree by his string, there is a painted tile of the Luxo ball on the wall behind him.

> *Did you know?*
>
> The bee on Bonnie's backpack is a character from the 1984 Pixar short, The Adventures of Andre and Wally B.

552. As the toys take their places in the caterpillar room for playtime, a toy hops away to hide under a bucket; which Pixar film is this toy from?
    - a. *The Incredibles*
    - b. *Cars*
    - c. *Monsters Inc.*
    - d. *A Bug's Life*

> *Did you know?*
>
> As the children run into the caterpillar room from the playground, one of the children is wearing a Lightning McQueen T-shirt.

553. Which toy does the child use as a paintbrush during playtime?
    - a. Jessie
    - b. Bullseye
    - c. Rex
    - d. Slinky dog

554. When Bonnie is playing tea party with her toys, what does she place in front of Trixie to use as a cup?
    a. Plastic cup
    b. Sippy cup
    c. Egg carton
    d. Cereal bowl

555. What is the shape of Buttercup, the unicorn's nostrils?
    a. Rainbows
    b. Hearts
    c. Stars
    d. Circles

556. What is Bonnie's secret ingredient in the hamburger she serves the toys for lunch?
    a. Sweet tarts
    b. Bubble gum
    c. Jelly beans
    d. Jawbreakers

Did you know?

The gray rabbit toy next to Bonnie's bed is Totoro, from the 1988 Japanese animated film *My Neighbor Totoro*.

557. When the toys are gambling at the top of the vending machine, what do they use as money?
    a. Exact Change® money
    b. Pay Day® money
    c. The Game of Life® money
    d. Monopoly® money

558. Which animal sound does Ken say is wild during the next round of gambling?
    a. Coyote
    b. Chicken
    c. Pig
    d. Donkey

Did you know?

When Lotso's henchmen take the cover off of Buzz Lightyears battery compartment, the batteries are Buy N Large, the brand found in the movie *WALL-E*.

559. How do Lotso and his henchmen change Buzz to control him?
  - a. Remove his wiring
  - b. Take out his batteries
  - c. Remove his helmet
  - d. Switch him to demo mode

560. What game are Hamm, Slinky Dog, and Mr. Potato Head playing while they wait for Buzz to return?
  - a. Checkers
  - b. Domino's
  - c. Yahtzee
  - d. Jacks

561. How do the toys figure out that Andy meant to put them in the attic?
  - a. Mr. Potato Head's lost eye
  - b. Mr. Potato Head's lost ear
  - c. Mrs. Potato Head's lost eye
  - d. Mrs. Potato Head's lost ear

562. What accessory does Barbie take from Ken when she realizes he is not a good guy?
  - a. Her scarf
  - b. Her scrunchie
  - c. Her leg warmers
  - d. Her earrings

563. When Buzz Lightyear refers to the box, what area is he referring to?
    a. Cardboard box
    b. Wading pool
    c. Sandbox
    d. Plastic storage container

Did you know?

The name Velocistar237 on the computer chat is a subtle reference to the film *The Shining*. In this movie, room 237 is a significant plot point.

Did you know?

The coins near the computer monitor create a hidden Mickey when Woody is typing.

564. When Woody finds where Andy's house is located on the computer and imagines himself at college, what does one of Bonnie's toys call him?
    a. Ralph
    b. Potsie
    c. Richie
    d. Fonzie

565. What is the name of the clown toy that shares Lotso's sordid past with Woody?
    a. Sprinkles
    b. Chuckles
    c. Twinkles
    d. Sparkles

> **Did you know?**
>
> After Lotso, Big Baby, and the clown toy find out Daisy has replaced Lotso, they ride on the bumper of the Pizza Planet truck.

566. Which of the imprisoned toys plays the harmonica while in his cell?
    a. Slinky dog
    b. Jessie
    c. Mr. Potato Head
    d. Hamm

> **Did you know?**
>
> As Woody sneaks back to Sunnyside and enters the caterpillar room through the ceiling tile, the letters on the wall spell out Atta. This is a reference to the Princess in *A Bug's Life*.

567. How does Slinky Dog tie up the mechanical monkey in the surveillance room?
    a. His coils
    b. Yarn
    c. Tape
    d. Gum

568. What food item does Mr. Potato Head attach his parts to when he escapes the playground?
    a. Tortilla
    b. Piece of bread
    c. Cracker
    d. Fruit roll

569. Which of these is *not* one of the toys that ride on Bullseye's back to escape the daycare center?
    a. Mrs. Potato Head
    b. Jessie
    c. The aliens
    d. Rex

570. What does Barbie use to tie up Ken while she destroys his wardrobe?
    a. Yarn
    b. Jump rope
    c. Paddleball
    d. His fringe jacket

571. Which of these is *not* one of the outfits Barbie destroys to try to get Ken to talk?
    a. Silver space suit
    b. Swim trunks
    c. Glitter tuxedo
    d. Nehru jacket

572. What language does Buzz Lightyear begin speaking after Rex holds down his reset button too long?
    a. Spanish
    b. Japanese
    c. French
    d. German

573. What type of flower does Buzz present to Jessie as he dances the flamenco around her?
    a. Foxglove
    b. Daisy
    c. Dandelion
    d. Forget me not

574. Which toy did Lotso and his henchmen break to find out about the escape plan?
    a. Barbie
    b. Toy telephone
    c. Mechanical monkey
    d. Big baby

575. What pattern adorns Ken's shorts as he runs to save Barbie from Lotso?
    a. Polka dots
    b. Stars
    c. Rainbows
    d. Hearts

576. What object is dropped on Buzz Lightyear that brings his memory back?
    a. VCR
    b. Television
    c. Toaster oven
    d. Stereo

577. What object does Rex hold onto when the magnet picks up the metal at the dump?
    a. Lunchbox
    b. Fan
    c. Cheese grater
    d. Hammer

578. Who saves the toys from the furnace at the dump?
    a. Big baby
    b. The aliens
    c. Lotso
    d. Barbie

579. What does Slinky Dog say he would like to do to Lotso after the toys are safe?
    a. Remove his glass eyes
    b. Give him a new scent
    c. Loosen his stitching
    d. Take out his stuffing

580. How does Mr. Potato Head drain the water from inside his potato after the toys get clean?
    a. Takes off his hat
    b. Takes off his ear
    c. Takes off his mustache
    d. Takes off his nose

Did you know?

The toys at Sunnyside daycare center play with the Luxo ball in the sandbox during the credits.

Did you know?

Toy Story 3 was the most expensive Pixar movie to date, with a cost of over two hundred million dollars. This was also the first Pixar film to gross over one billion dollars worldwide.

Cars 2

581. When the agent is sending his transmission to Fin McMissile, that shape does he state his mission has gone?

    a. Pickle   c. Pear

    b. Plum   d. Peach

582. When Crabby gets caught by the combat ship, he tells the ship, "Don't get your _____ in a twist."

    a. Prop   c. Radar

    b. Flags   d. Steel

Did you know?

Finn McMissile's license plate includes the numbers 314, Michael Kaine's birthday. Caine is the voice of Finn McMissle.

583. When Finn McMissle scans the ship, what is Professor Zundapp's profession?

    a. Industrial spy   c. Car parts expert

    b. Linguist   d. Weapons designer

584. When Mater finds Otis by the side of the road, what does Otis say his starter is as smooth as?
    a. Jelly
    c. Oil
    b. Butter
    d. Pudding

> *Did you know?*
>
> Character actor Jeff Garlin voices Otis; you may recognize him as the captain's voice in *WALL-E* and Buttercup in *Toy Story 3*.

585. As Lightning McQueen is reminiscing in Doc Hudson's office, how many racing wins did Doc Hudson take him in 1951?
    a. Twenty-two
    c. Thirteen
    b. Twenty-three
    d. Sixteen

586. What movie is playing at the Radiator Springs Drive-in Theater when Mater and Lightning McQueen drive by?
    a. Finding Nismo
    c. Christine
    b. The Incredimobiles
    d. Grand Torino

587. What was Mater's favorite new souvenir of his day out with Lightning McQueen
    a. His new paint job
    c. His new dent
    b. His new balloon
    d. His new headlights

588. What is the name of the newspaper with the head-line "Billionaire Mission"?
    a. Rearview Mirror
    b. Windshield of the World
    c. Tracking through Tires
    d. Rear Bumper

589. What is the flight number for Tokyo Japan at the international terminal?
    a. 814
    b. 741
    c. A113
    d. 324

Did you know?

The movie Lightning McQueen and Mater are watching on the plane to Tokyo is the car version of Takeshi's Castle, a popular game show.

Did you know?

The Mount Fuji snow runoff is in the shape of car treads.

590. When Lightning McQueen and Mater arrive in Tokyo, what product is being advertised with Lightning's face?
    a. Mop
    b. Vacuum
    c. Broom
    d. Car wash

591. What car part does the red car buy from the vending machine in Tokyo?
    a. Hub caps
    b. Tires
    c. Oil
    d. Headlights

> *Did you know?*
>
> When Mater and Lightning McQueen get into the elevator, the lift is a car piston.

592. When agent Shipwell finds Finn McMissle at the World Grand Prix's reception, what part does she say a Carmen Gia does not have?
    a. Fuel injection
    b. Crankcase
    c. Battery
    d. Radiator

593. What does Mater assume is pistachio ice cream at the World Grand Prix reception?
    a. Green tea ice cream
    b. Mochi
    c. Wasabi
    d. Sushi

594. The two cars that go into the restroom to rough up the spy are a Pacer, and what other car model?
    a. Fiero
    b. Pinto
    c. Yugo
    d. Gremlin

595. What is the real purpose of the camera Professor Zundap brought to the World Grand Prix?
    a. Electromagnetic Pulse
    b. Atom bomb
    c. Hydrogen bomb
    d. Hypnosis machine

596. Which of these is *not* one of the commentators at the World Grand Prix in Tokyo?
    a. Brent Mustangburger
    b. Darrell Cartrip
    c. John Drippan
    d. David Hobbscap

> **Did you know?**
>
> After the race starts, the crews can be seen. Jeff Govette's crew chief is the voice of director John Lassiter.

> **Did you know?**
>
> The famous Tokyo Rainbow Bridge is made up of car parts.

597. Which is the first car to be taken out of the race by the electromagnetic pulse camera?
    a. Carla Veloso
    b. Raoul CaRoule
    c. Miguel Camino
    d. Jeff Gorvette

598. Which of these is Acer, the evil Pacer's correct VIN number?
    a. A58667A372159   c. A76685A951273
    b. A372159A58667   d. A951273A76685

599. What does Mater like to have done before meeting a lady friend?
    a. Fill his tires with   c. Brush his grill
       air   d. Proper detailing
    b. Full tank of gas

600. What does Mater check his reflection with as he leaves Lightning McQueen's pit area?
    a. Tool chest   c. Garage door
    b. Car hood   d. Crescent wrench

601. What does Finn McMissle use to stop the two henchmen from getting to Mater?
    a. Motor oil   c. Windshield
    b. Fire extinguisher   wiper fluid
                               d. Tire air

602. During the fight in the alley, what is seen in the chopsticks on the billboard just before the car flies up to take its place?
    a. Hubcap   c. Nut
    b. Bolt   d. Rearview mirror

Did you know?

Finn McMissile's plane has the number A113 on the tail wing. This is a reference to the Cal Arts classroom where the animators for Pixar went to school. The British Intelligence seal has the Latin phrase, "Honor, Animus, Vis Equorum." Translated to English, this reads "Honor, Spirit, Horsepower."

603. What is the name of the hotel the stationary Mater writes his goodbye letter to Lightning McQueen on?
    a. V8 Hotel   c. Hot Wheels hotel
    b. Motor 6   d. Imerawheel
                                Hotel

604. After Finn McMissle and Mater board his private plane, finish the following statement by Finn, "You never feel more alive than when you are almost _____."
    a. Shot   c. Run over
    b. Dead   d. Totaled

Did you know?

When Mater arrives in Paris, they drive by Gastow's Restaurant. This is a nod to Gasteau's in *Ratatouille*.

605. What make and model is the three-wheel car Tomber Finn McMissle chases in Paris?
    a. Reliant Regal   c. Morgan
    b. Mazda K360   d. Benz Motorwagon

606. When Mater tows Tomber into the garage, what does Tomber say he has never liked?
    a. Rookies
    b. New car smell
    c. Flashy body styles
    d. Rusty engines

Did you know?

When Lightning McQueen stays with Luigi's family, he has a cousin named Topolino. This is the name used for Mickey Mouse in Italy.

---

607. As Mater tests the voice-controlled disguise software, what monster does he appear to be when he asks the computer to make him a monster truck?
    a. Dracula
    b. Frankenstein
    c. The wolfman
    d. The mummy

608. What part of Mater does he tell Holly is much too valuable to change?
    a. His engine
    b. His tow hook
    c. His headlights
    d. His dents

609. What Holly Shiftwell's career did she use as a cover?
    a. Tech support engineer
    b. Web design
    c. Designing Iphone™ apps
    d. Database consultant

> *Did you know?*
>
> The rock shape in Porto Corsa is in the shape of the Fiat 500 Topolino. The Marina is in the shape of a wheel.

610. Which car is in third place behind Lightning McQueen at the beginning of the second leg of the World Grand Prix?
    a. Shu Todoroki
    b. Carla Veloso
    c. Nigel Gearsley
    d. Shifty Cadillacson

> *Did you know?*
>
> The dice used at the craps table in the casino are fuzzy dice on a cord. These dice are seen hanging from rearview mirrors, popular in the 1950s.

611. What items sit in the center of the table during the meeting with the big boss in the casino?
    a. Candelabras
    b. Flowers
    c. Lemons
    d. Oranges

612. What does the big boss give as the reason he could not be at the meeting in person?
    a. His clutch assembly broke
    b. His drive train broke
    c. His axle broke
    d. He has flat tires

613. When Carla Veloso crashes on the casino bridge, from which country does she originate?
    a. France
    c. Germany
    b. Italy
    d. Brazil

614. When Mater escapes from the meeting and tries to warn Lightning McQueen that they are trying to kill him, what do the guards at the gate call him?
    a. Lunatic
    c. Imbecile
    b. Crazy car
    d. Insane

Did you know?

There is an advertisement for Lassetyre at the London leg of the World Grand Prix. This is a nod to director John Lassiter, head of Pixar.

615. What advertisement is to the right of the Lassetyre ad on the track in London?
    a. UK Motor Lube
    c. Royal Radiators
    b. Rostyle
    d. Petrolla

616. What part of Mater is left behind in Big Bentley after he makes his escape?
    a. Oil pan
    c. Air filter
    b. Gas cap
    d. Dipstick

617. What is advertised on the double-decker bus that the cars almost crash into while the professor is trying to escape?

    a. Castro's

    b. Calahan's

    c. Cashington

    d. Carlo's

Did you know?

The advertisement on the side of Topper Deckington is a tribute to lightning director Sharon Calahan.

618. What is the name of the pub where the two henchmen crash after Holly stops them from trying to kill Lightening McQueen?

    a. Ye Three Point Turn Inn

    b. Ye Right Turn Inn

    c. Ye U-Turn Inn

    d. Ye Left Turn Inn

Did you know?

A tapestry inside the pub is a car representation of the royal family in Brave, the next Pixar film to be released.

619. Who saves Lightning McQueen and Mater from the professor and his henchmen when they are trapped at the intersection?

    a. Red the firetruck

    b. Sally Carrera

    c. Filmore

    d. Sarge

620. What type of cars are guarding the Queen during the race?
    a. Mercedes Benz   c. BMW
    b. Range Rovers   d. Porches

621. When the bomb is deactivated, what does the read-out say after?
    a. You are the bomb   c. Have a nice day
    b. Pleasure doing   d. Ta ta
       business

622. Who sends the email to Finn McMissle to come to Radiator Springs?
    a. Sally   c. Fillmore
    b. Sarge   d. Luigi

623. Who switched out Lightning McQueen's fuel for Fillmore's organic fuel at the race?
    a. Mater   c. Sarge
    b. Fillmore   d. Luigi

Did you know?

The Pizza Planet truck can be seen watching the final race on the right-side bear of Pop N Patch Tire Repair.

Did you know?

During the credits, there is an advertisement for Air Uxo; the Luxo lamp is the logo for the airline.

Did you know?

Mater's birthday on his passport is a nod to director John Lassiter; they share a birthday.

Brave

Did you know?

Brave is the first Pixar film to be set in a time in the past.

624. What country does the movie *Brave* take place in?
    a. Scotland
    b. Ireland
    c. England
    d. Finland

625. What sort of birds sit on the perches as Queen Elinor searches for Merida?
    a. Eagles
    b. Falcons
    c. Vultures
    d. Hawks

626. What special day are the royal family celebrating at the beginning of the film?
    a. The King's birthday
    b. Christmas
    c. Merida's birthday
    d. Thanksgiving

627. What are the blue flames Merida sees in the forest when she retrieves the arrow called?
    a. Blarney wisps
    b. Will O' the wisps
    c. Heather wisps
    d. Blue wisps

628. What does Queen Elinor claim the wisps lead you to?
    a. Your fate
    b. Your destiny
    c. Your doom
    d. Your true love

Did you know?

The loops of Queen Elinor's belt create a hidden Mickey

629. What weapon do King Fergus and his guards use to fight off the bear that comes into their camp?
    a. Whips
    b. Bow and arrows
    c. Clubs
    d. Spears

630. What part of King Fergus's body does he lose to the demon bear?
    a. Leg
    b. Arm
    c. Nose
    d. Pinky finger

631. Which of these is *not* one of the names of Merida's brothers?
    a. Hubert
    b. Hamish
    c. Harold
    d. Harris

632. What piece of fruit is Merida eating when the doors of the castle open to reveal her?
    a. Orange   c. Apple
    b. Pear   d. Fig

633. As Queen Elinor teaches Merida to be a proper Princess, what does she say a princess must be knowledgeable about?
    a. Her history   c. Her manners
    b. Her kingdom   d. Her family

634. What is the name of the small harp Merida is learning to play during her lessons?
    a. Mandolin   c. Lyre
    b. Lute   d. Zither

635. When Merida laughs at the falconry lesson, what does Queen Elinor tell her a princess does not do?
    a. Giggle   c. Snigger
    b. Chuckle   d. Chortle

636. As Merida's brother eat their breakfast, what does Queen Elinor tell them not to play with?
    a. Their haggis   c. Their black
    b. Their porridge   pudding
                        d. Their kippers

637. What does Merida strike her sword against in her bedroom to show her frustration?
    a. Her bedpost   c. Her vanity
    b. Her dresser   d. Her candelabra

Did you know?

As Queen Elinor creates the needlepoint of her daughter Merida on the tapestry, she shows Merida with her hair pulled back the same style as her own instead of how Merida's hair is usually worn.

638. When King Fergus enters the bed-chamber, he tells Queen Elinor she is doing what?
    a. Grumbling
    b. Singing
    c. Sighing
    d. Muttering

639. What is the name of Merida's horse she talks to in the stables?
    a. Graeme
    b. Malcolm
    c. Tavish
    d. Angus

640. What does Merida's brother do to the sleeping guard at the festival?
    a. Cut off half of his mustache
    b. Tie is shoelaces together
    c. Stick a firecracker in his kilt
    d. Steal his spear

641. Which of these is *not* the name of the clans presenting their suitors?
    a. Macintosh
    b. MacDonald
    c. MacGuffin
    d. Dingwall

642. What does Lord MacGuffin's son break between his hands to show his strength?
   a. A bagpipe
   b. A rock
   c. A log
   d. A candle

643. How many Romans was Lord Dingwall's son besieged by in battle?
   a. Seven hundred
   b. Ten million
   c. Two thousand
   d. Ten thousand

644. When the Lords are taunting each other, what does Lord Macintosh call Lord Dingwall?
   a. Goblin
   b. Troll
   c. Witch
   d. Gnome

645. How does Lord Dingwall's son attack Lord Macintosh?
   a. Bites him
   b. Punches him
   c. Pinches him
   d. Slaps him

646. How does Queen Elinor stop the Lords from fighting each other?
   a. Stares them down
   b. Pinches them on the arms
   c. Yells at them
   d. Grabs them by the ears

647. What sort of creatures is made of straw for the children to hit during the festival?
   a. Horse
   b. Moose
   c. Sheep
   d. Bear

648. As Merida and her mother argue in Merida's bedroom, what does Queen Elinor throw into the fire?
    a. Her clothes
    b. The tapestry
    c. Her bow
    d. Her necklace

649. How many stones create the circle Merida lands in when Angus throws her from his back?
    a. Twelve
    b. Fourteen
    c. Ten
    d. Seventeen

> *Did you know?*
>
> As Merida walks up to the woodcarver's home, the address is A113 in roman numerals.

650. As Merida enters the woodcarvers, how much does the carver tell her everything is on sale?
    a. One hundred percent
    b. Ten percent
    c. Twenty percent
    d. Half

651. What is Merida's first hint that the woodcarver is a witch within the woodcarver's house?
    a. The broom sweeps by itself
    b. The chisel continues carving
    c. The wood chips put themselves in the trash
    d. The shelves dust themselves

> *Did you know?*
>
> As Merida realizes the woodcarver is a witch, you can see the Pizza Planet truck briefly on the table in front of the piece the witch is carving.

> *Did you know?*
>
> There is a carving of a bear in the shape of The Thinker sitting atop the table the witch stands behind.

> *Did you know?*
>
> The Luxo ball can be seen as the witch threatens Merida with the knives. It is very difficult to see, but the ball sits within a box.

652. What does Merida offer to buy if she can get a spell from the witch?
    - a. One of each carving
    - b. Everything
    - c. One carving
    - d. Half of everything

> *Did you know?*
>
> As Merida's gaze sweeps over the items in the woodcarvers' home, there is a carving of Sully from Monster's Inc. sitting on the floor.

> *Did you know?*
>
> The witch holds up a board with a carving of the Hand of God with bears.

653. Who was the last person the witch conjured for as she steps into her house again?
    a. A troll
    b. A king
    c. A queen
    d. A Prince

654. What did the Prince give the witch in payment for his spell?
    a. A gold coin
    b. A necklace
    c. A ring
    d. A crown

655. What form does the spell the witch created for Merida take?
    a. A tart
    b. A pie
    c. A pudding
    d. Haggis

656. How long does the witch tell Merida to expect delivery of her spell?
    a. A mensem
    b. A fortnight
    c. A millennium
    d. A week

657. What sort of fruit does Merida place on the plate with the tart?
    a. Blueberries
    b. Strawberries
    c. Raspberries
    d. Boysenberries

658. When Queen Elinor eats a piece of the tart, how does she describe the taste?
    a. Gamey
    b. Sweet
    c. Interesting
    d. Savory

659. How does King Fergus know there is a bear in the castle?
    a. His leg aches
    b. He smells it
    c. His guard tells him
    d. He senses it

660. What is Merida's brother using as a bear head when they see their mother for the first time as a bear?
    a. Sheep
    b. Skunk
    c. Rabbit
    d. Deer

661. What does Merida offer her brothers to help get their mother out of the castle safely?
    a. Her toys
    b. Her breakfast
    c. Her desserts
    d. Her bedroom

662. What animal on a stick does Merida's brother use to distract King Fergus?
    a. Snake
    b. Lizard
    c. Frog
    d. Gopher

663. What do the Lords and their men use as a rope to climb down from the roof of the castle?
    a. Ropes
    b. Tapestries
    c. Banners
    d. Their kilts

664. As Merida enters the witches' house and the automated message starts, which vial does she need to throw into the cauldron to tell the witch she is there?
    a. Vial 2
    b. Vial 3
    c. Vial 4
    d. Vial 1

665. When the witch automated message addresses Merida, when does she say she will be returning?
    a. Spring
    b. Summer
    c. Winter
    d. Fall

666. How long does Merida have to undo the spell cast on her mother, according to the witch?
    a. The next full moon
    b. The third sundown
    c. The second sunrise
    d. The end of the week

667. As Merida reminisces about her mother, what does her mother comfort Merida through as a toddler?
    a. Wild animals
    b. Lightning
    c. Shadows
    d. Darkness

668. What does Queen Elinor serve for breakfast the morning after the rainstorm?
    a. Elderberries
    b. Holly berries
    c. White baneberries
    d. Nightshade berries

669. As Queen Elinor tries to wash the berries out of her mouth, what does Merida say it is in the water?
    a. Algae
    b. Worms
    c. Spiders
    d. Flies

670. As Queen Elinor eats the fish, what does she use as a napkin?
    a. Merida's gown
    b. Her gown
    c. A leaf
    d. A twig

671. Which of the four Princes in the ancient story split the stone and became a bear?
    a. The elders
    b. The youngest
    c. The second
    d. The third

672. How do Merida and Queen Elinor sneak back into the castle?
    a. Over the wall
    b. Through a secret passage
    c. Through the gates
    d. Through a well

673. What does Merida use to pry the door open when her father locks her in to save her from the bear?
    a. Broom handle
    b. Shovel
    c. Fire poker
    d. Tapestry hook

674. Who gets the key for Merida when she is locked in the room?
    a. The maid
    b. Her brothers
    c. The guards
    d. King Fergus

675. What does the maid use to protect herself from Merida's brothers?
    a. Frying pan
    b. A spoon
    c. A broom
    d. A mop

676. Who saves Merida from Mor 'du?
    a. Her father
    b. Her mother
    c. Her brothers
    d. The clans

677. Who stows away aboard one of the departing ships?
    a. Queen Elinor
    b. Merida
    c. Merida's brothers
    d. King Fergus

Monsters University

678. What is the name of the elementary school Mike attends as a child?
    a. Scaryville Elementary
    b. Frighton Elementary
    c. Monsters Elementary
    d. Little Scarers Elementary

679. Which of these is *not* one of the rules the teacher gives when the class arrives for their field trip?
    a. No disappearing
    b. No fire breathing
    c. No pushing
    d. No biting

680. What item does Mike find on the bus when the teacher forgets him?
    a. A dollar
    b. A quarter
    c. A penny
    d. A nickel

681. As Frank McKay is in the child's bedroom with Mike, the bedroom door opens, and Mike hides on a wall hook. What sort of hat is perched on top of the wooden rocking horse in front of Frank?
    a. Top hat
    b. Baseball cap
    c. Cowboy hat
    d. Football helmet

> *Did you know?*
>
> The Monsters University campus was designed to resemble the University of California Berkley. The Monsters University gates were modeled after Sather Gate.

682. As Mike arrives at Monsters University and begins his checklist, what is the fourth item on his list?
    a. Eat
    b. Hang posters
    c. Ace my classes
    d. Become a scarer

683. While on the orientation tour, Mike visits the cafeteria. What is advertised on the large banner on the wall behind the buffet?
    a. First scare dance
    b. First-semester bonfire
    c. First freshman BBQ
    d. First-day dinner

684. When Mike receives the flyer for the scare games, what is the final sign-up date?
    a. January 25
    b. March 13
    c. August 14
    d. December 2

685. What is Mike's room number when he arrives at the dorm?

   a. 139   c. 319

   b. A113   d. 931

Did you know?

The dorm room on the second floor is room 319. This references the 2319 emergency code in the first Monsters Inc. film when the sock is found on George Sanderson.

---

686. As Mike and Randall meet and talk in the hallway, a new student carries boxes down the hall behind them. What unusual item is he carrying on the top box?

   a. A parrot cage   c. A Santa Claus hat

   b. A small dog   d. Pink flamingos

Did you know?

Mike suggests to Randall that he remove his glasses when he disappears. This creates the squinting eyes that we see in the first Monsters Inc. film.

---

687. As Mike and Randall unpack, what is the time on the digital clock Randall sets on the table?

   a. 9:15   c. 8:14

   b. 12:45   d. 12:02

> *Did you know?*
>
> There is a poster on Randall's side of the dorm room that reads, "The winds of change: Shh, can you hear them? This is a reference to *Monsters Inc.*, in which Randall says this to Mike at the beginning of the workday.

> *Did you know?*
>
> As the scare students enter the building, they each touch the paw of the monster statue. This is a reference to the tradition at Harvard University in which each student touches the foot of founder John Harvard for good luck.

688. What does Dean Hardscrabble tell the students is the true mark of a monster?
    - a. Terror
    - b. Roaring
    - c. Looks
    - d. Scariness

> *Did you know?*
>
> The classroom number is A113; this refers to the animation classroom at Cal Arts, where most of the Pixar animators went to school.

689. What is the name of the monster pig Sulley chases into Mike's room?
    a. Mickey
    b. Archie
    c. Tully
    d. Lily

Did you know?

The Pizza Planet truck is parked outside the fraternity house when Mike and Sulley are chasing the pig.

690. When Mike chases the pig into the fraternity house, there is a street sign on the wall above a doorway. What is the street name on this sign?
    a. Mockingbird Land
    b. Howl street
    c. Cemetery Lane
    d. Psycho street

691. When Mike is reading the chapter on the Cobra Hiss, how many degrees is the brow inversion on the diagram?
    a. 160
    b. 90
    c. 102
    d. 30

692. What is the name of the floor buffing machine Mike rides during his work-study program?
    a. BUFFMaster
    b. Buff Monster
    c. Buff Buster
    d. Buff Builder

693. What does Sulley trip over when he knocks Dean Hardscrabble's canister off its pedestal?
     a. A jacket
     b. A pencil
     c. A book
     d. A chair

694. After Mike is removed from the scaring program, what class does he take after the break?
     a. Sidekick studies
     b. Door carpentry
     c. Mailroom sorting
     d. Scream can design

> *Did you know?*
>
> When Mike and Sulley arrive at the Oozma Kappa fraternity house, there is a hidden Mickey in the pattern on the couch in the living room.

695. When Mike and Sulley arrive at the Oozma Kappa fraternity house, what industry does Frank tell them he was in for thirty years?
     a. Data processing
     b. Flooring
     c. Pharmaceuticals
     d. Textiles

> *Did you know?*
>
> The area code of the phone number of Don's card is 510; this is the area code for Emeryville, Ca. where Pixar headquarters is located.

696. What is Art's major in college?
    a. Underwater basket weaving
    b. New age philosophy
    c. Women's studies
    d. History of scaring

697. After the initiation, what do the brothers build a fort out of?
    a. Sheets
    b. Blankets
    c. Couch cushions
    d. Furniture

Did you know?

As Mike talks in his sleep, he says, "I know you are a princess, and I am just a stable boy." This is a reference to the film *The Princess Bride,* in which Billy Crystal makes a cameo.

698. What does Sulley scream out after he falls out of bed after the alarm goes off?
    a. Mom
    b. Dad
    c. Mike
    d. Roar

699. Which of these is *not* one of the fraternities or sororities competing in the scare games?
    a. Python Nu Kappa
    b. Jaws Omega Roar
    c. Eta Hiss Hiss
    d. Slugma Slugma Kappa

> *Did you know?*
>
> There is a drawing of the Luxo Jr. ball on the wall of the sewer at the beginning of the scare games.

700. What is used during the scare games to simulate a child's toy?
    - a. Poisonous octopus tentacles
    - b. Monster snake venom
    - c. Stinging glow urchins
    - d. Lava starfish

701. When the rest of the Oozma Kappa team crosses the finish line, what does Squishy say he cannot feel?
    - a. His body
    - b. His soul
    - c. His toes
    - d. His everything

702. What is the reason Jaws Theta Kai was eliminated from the scare games?
    - a. Bypassing the designated course route
    - b. Use of illegal protective gel
    - c. Flying over the course
    - d. Not participating in the event

703. What is the strength of Terry and Terri from Oozma Kappa?
    - a. A loud roar
    - b. Sneaking
    - c. They have an extra toe
    - d. Close up magic

704. Which member of Oozma Kappa does Mike say they need to get a bell for?
    a. Squishy
    b. Terry and Terri
    c. Don
    d. Art

705. Which member of Oozma Kappa retrieves the flag from the library during the second event?
    a. Art
    b. Don
    c. Squishy
    d. Sulley

> **Did you know?**
>
> During the third challenge, the scarers are running through a maze to avoid the teenagers. One of the voices can be heard saying, "But daddy, I love him." This is a reference to Ariel in *The Little Mermaid*.

706. When the guys from Oozma Kappa look in at Monster Inc., which scarer is at the top of the leader board on the scare floor?
    a. Benitez
    b. Thompson
    c. Gutierrez
    d. Gunderson

707. Which of Oozma Kappa members says he cannot go back to prison when they get caught by the guards at Monsters Inc.?
    a. Squishy
    b. Art
    c. Don
    d. Mike

708. When Oozma Kappa's members run from the guards at Monster Inc, what does Squishy's mom offer the boys when they get back in the car?
    a. Mints
    b. Candy
    c. Gum
    d. Cookies

709. As Sulley and Randall enter the scare simulator, what design appears on Randall when he falls after Sulley's roar?
    a. Hearts
    b. Flowers
    c. Stars
    d. Polka dots

710. Which member of Roar Omega Roar competes against Mike in the scare simulator?
    a. Chip Goff
    b. Randall Boggs
    c. Worthington
    d. Reggie Jacobs

711. When Mrs. Squibbles meets Don after the scare games, what does she reveal is her first name?
    a. Carrie
    b. Terry
    c. Mary
    d. Sherry

712. After Mike breaks into the door lab and attempts to scare a child, what is her reaction to Mike?
    a. "You're not scary."
    b. "You look funny."
    c. "You're adorable."
    d. "Eeek"

713. What is the name of the camp Mike finds himself in when he walks through the door?
    a. Camp Wannahockalugi
    b. Camp Teamwork
    c. Camp Inch
    d. Camp Leadership

714. When Mike and Sulley try to get back to the monster world, what do they find when they open the door?
    a. A closet
    b. A bathroom
    c. Outside
    d. A kitchen

715. When the police enter the cabin to investigate, what toy moves across the floor?
    a. A puppy
    b. A truck
    c. A doll
    d. A ball

716. When the CDC arrives at the university, what is the number of the first CDC member to enter the door lab?
    a. 04114
    b. 01441
    c. 01414
    d. 04141

Did you know?

Roz makes an appearance with the CDC at the university. She can be heard saying her famous line, "We are always watching."

717. After Mike stops the bus to talk to Sulley, Dean Hardscrabble arrives to show them the campus newspaper. She explains to the boys that they have done something no one has ever been able to do before. What did they do?
    a. Prove her wrong
    b. Scare her
    c. Impress her
    d. Surprise her

718. When Mike and Sulley get a job in the mailroom at Monsters Inc., who is their supervisor?
    a. Mr. Waternoose
    b. Roz
    c. The abominable snowman
    d. Randall

719. When Mike opens his locker, what does the newspaper's headline read just above the plaque in his locker?
    a. Meet your new janitorial team
    b. CDC offers reward for child capture
    c. Monsters University scandal
    d. Bring your pet monster to workday

Did you know?

Inside Mike's lockers, several sticky notes read, "File paperwork." This is a reference to Mike's inability to file his paperwork in *Monsters Inc.*

Inside Out

720. How long were Riley and Joy together before Sadness comes along?
   a. Thirty-three hours
   b. Thirty-three seconds
   c. Thirty-three days
   d. Thirty hours

> **Did you know?**
>
> Joy is the only emotion that does not cast a shadow. This is due to her shining personality.

721. What vegetable is in Riley's bowl when she is sitting in her high chair?
   a. Spinach
   b. Broccoli
   c. Carrots
   d. Peas

722. What does the headline read on the newspaper Anger is reading?
   a. No dessert
   b. No broccoli
   c. Time Out
   d. Bedtime

723. What part of Riley's memory powers the Personality Islands?
     a. Angry memories
     b. Joyful memories
     c. Core memories
     d. Powerful memories

724. What does Riley's dad call her when he is chasing her through the house after bath time?
     a. Princess
     b. Silly
     c. Goofball
     d. Monkey

725. How does Fear measure a successful day?
     a. They are happy
     b. They did not get hurt
     c. They did not get into trouble
     d. They did not die

726. What is the name of the moving company that helps Riley's family move from their home?
     a. National Movers
     b. Lightning Movers
     c. Lightyear Movers
     d. Lassiter Movers

Did you know?

As Riley's family is driving, you can catch a glimpse of the birds from the Pixar short, For the Birds sitting on the telephone wire above the road.

> **Did you know?**
>
> The dinosaur statue that Riley's family takes pictures in front of resembles the dinosaur from the forthcoming Pixar film *The Good Dinosaur*.

727. Which of these is *not* one of the houses Riley imagines her family will live in?
    a. Gingerbread house
    b. Castle
    c. Dollhouse
    d. Treehouse

728. When Riley explores the new house, what disease does Fear claim they will get?
    a. The plague
    b. Rabies
    c. Salmonella
    d. Lyme disease

729. What sort of curtains does Joy claim will fix Riley's room?
    a. Kitty
    b. Flowers
    c. Butterfly
    d. Bird

730. Which day of the week will the moving van arrive at the new house?
    a. Thursday
    b. Friday
    c. Monday
    d. Saturday

731. What does Riley's dad use as a hockey stick when the family moves into their new house?
    a. A shovel
    b. A broom
    c. A rake
    d. A mop

732. How do Riley's memories change from happy to sad?
    a. Anger touches them
    b. Sadness touches them
    c. Disgust touches them
    d. Joy forgets they are happy memories

Did you know?

Some of Riley's memory balls contain scenes from other Pixar films. One ball contains the wedding scene from *Up*.

Did you know?

There are three buttons on the top console that create a hidden Mickey.

733. How does Joy distract Sadness from obsessing?
    a. Reading mind manuals
    b. Cleaning up the old memories
    c. Creating new sad memories
    d. Taking a nap

734. When Riley is lying in bed, she sees car headlights on the bedroom wall. What does fear think this is?
    a. A bear
    b. A robber
    c. A lion
    d. A tiger

735. When the emotions are arguing about the move, how many things does Fear tell the others Riley needs to be afraid of?
    a. Thirty-five
    b. Thirty-three
    c. Thirty-seven
    d. Thirty-nine

736. After Riley falls asleep, which emotion has dream duty?
    a. Disgust
    b. Fear
    c. Anger
    d. Joy

Did you know?

When Riley dreams about the broccoli pizza, you can hear the Haunted Mansion theme in the background.

737. What is the name of the breakfast cereal Riley eats before her first day of school?
    a. Sugar Frosted Snaps
    b. Caramel Corn Curls
    c. Honey Nut O's
    d. Blue Berry Bows

Did you know?

The magazine sitting atop the card table features a photo of Collette from the Pixar film *Ratatouille* on the cover.

738. What instrument does Joy play when she wakes up
the other emotions?
    a. Trumpet
    b. Ukulele
    c. Accordion
    d. Bagpipes

> *Did you know?*
>
> As Riley is sitting in class waiting for the bell to ring, one
> of the cool girls is wearing the same T-shirt Sid wears in
> *Toy Story*.

739. When Fear brings in the potential disasters, which
of these is *not* one he mentions?
    a. Called on by the teacher
    b. Volcanic eruption
    c. Quicksand
    d. Spontaneous combustion

> *Did you know?*
>
> The classroom number is A113, the classroom at Cal Arts
> where the animators for Pixar went to school to learn
> the art of animation.

740. When the teacher asks Riley to tell the class about
Minnesota, how many compliment check marks
are there on the board?
    a. Five
    b. Eight
    c. Six
    d. Seven

> *Did you know?*
>
> The map on the wall of the classroom has pins marking specific cities. Each of these pins marks the location of the place where other Pixar films were set.

741. After Riley sits down, which book does the teacher tell the class to take out?
    - a. History
    - b. Geography
    - c. Math
    - d. English

742. Where do Joy and Sadness travel to when they get through the memory tubes?
    - a. Memory island
    - b. Islands of personality
    - c. Long term memory
    - d. Headquarters

> *Did you know?*
>
> The storage area for long-term memory curves into the natural folds of the brain.

743. When Riley's family is having dinner, what does her mother tell them the green trash can is used for?
    - a. Bottles only
    - b. Recycling
    - c. Trash
    - d. Greens

744. Which emotion is in charge of headquarters inside Riley's mothers' brain?
    - a. Anger
    - b. Joy
    - c. Sadness
    - d. Disgust

745. What are the emotions inside Riley's fathers' head doing when her mom tries to get his attention?
    a. Reading the newspaper
    b. Napping
    c. Watching hockey
    d. Working

746. What does Anger inside Riley's father's head threaten to do in response to Riley's anger?
    a. Send her to bed without dinner
    b. Yell
    c. Put her in her room
    d. Put his foot down

747. What is the name of the area below the islands of personality?
    a. Memory cavern
    b. Memory dump
    c. Memory pit
    d. Memory canyon

748. What is the map that will lead Joy and Sadness back to Headquarters?
    a. Sadness
    b. The manuals
    c. Core memories
    d. Instinct

749. How do the mind workers get rid of faded memories?
    a. Sweep them
    b. Vacuum them
    c. Shovel them
    d. Throw them

750. What is the memory that the mind workers send up to headquarters, forcing Riley to listen to over and over again?
    a. Tripledent gum
    b. Edger Manor bologna
    c. Presley chocolate
    d. McDowell's hamburgers

751. What is the name of Riley's imaginary friend?
    a. Elephaphin
    b. Ding Dong
    c. Bing Bong
    d. Dolphant

Did you know?

The flower petals on Bing Bong's flower are the same colors as the main emotions in Riley's headquarters.

752. What was the rocket Riley made with her imaginary friend made from?
    a. Bicycle
    b. Wagon
    c. Sled
    d. Scooter

753. Which of these is *not* one of the parts Bing Bong is made from?
    a. Cat
    b. Dolphin
    c. Elephant
    d. Hippopotamus

754. Which land does Bing Bong tell Joy and Sadness they can catch the train of thought?
    a. Inspiration land
    b. Creativity land
    c. Imagination land
    d. Vision land

755. How does Bing Bong spell shortcut?
    a. ESCAPE
    c. BEWARE
    b. WARNING
    d. DANGER

756. What sort of drink does Riley have on her lunch tray at the schoolyard?
    a. Apple juice
    c. Soda
    b. Milk
    d. Water

757. Which abstract through is the mind workers trying to comprehend today as they stand outside abstract thought?
    a. Fear
    c. Sadness
    b. Loneliness
    d. Anxiety

758. What is the forest in imagination land made from?
    a. Bacon
    c. Broccoli
    b. Asparagus
    d. French fries

Did you know?

In Imagination land, there is a stack of board games, and there is a game entitled "Find Me" with a picture of Nemo from *Finding Nemo* on the box.

759. Where does Bing Bong find the rocket he built with Riley?
    a. Puzzle pile
    c. Cloud town
    b. House of cards
    d. Preschool world

> *Did you know?*
>
> Figment from the ride Journey into Imagination with Figment at Epcot can be seen in one of the discarded memory orbs.

760. Which emotion tries to replace the core memories for hockey to help Riley?
    a. Anger
    b. Disgust
    c. Fear
    d. Sadness

> *Did you know?*
>
> The castle for princess dreamworld looks conspicuously like Cinderella Castle at Walt Disney World's Magic Kingdom.

761. What animal sits atop the stuff animal hall of fame?
    a. Unicorn
    b. Kitten
    c. Pony
    d. Teddy bear

> *Did you know?*
>
> During the flashbacks of Riley playing with Bing Bong, you can see the Luxo Jr. ball in the house.

762. Which emotion tries to quit?
    a. Fear
    b. Anger
    c. Disgust
    d. Sadness

763. Which one of these is *not* one of the movie posters on the soundstage in dream studios?
    a. I'm falling for a very long time into a pit
    b. Attack of the fluffy puppies
    c. I can fly
    d. Something's chasing me

Did you know?

One of the props in Dream Studios' backstage area is the giant monster's legs from *Monsters Inc.*

---

764. What sort of animal does Joy and Sadness dress as to wake Riley from sleep?
    a. Elephant
    b. Bear
    c. Horse
    d. Dog

765. Where do the security guards take Bing Bong?
    a. Sleeping island
    b. Left brain
    c. Subconscious
    d. Sandman studio

766. Which of these is *not* one of the dark fears Joy and Sadness encounter in Riley's subconscious?
    a. Neighbors big dog
    b. Grandma's vacuum
    c. Broccoli
    d. Stairs to the basement

767. What is Bing Bong's cage made from in the Subconscious?

    a. Clouds   c. Balloons

    b. Rocks   d. Glitter

Did you know?

Jangles the Clown is a tribute to animator Joe Ranft. Jangles is modeled after Ranft's Buttocks, the clown character that he occasionally dressed up as before his death.

768. How do Joy and Sadness get Jangles the clown to follow them to the dream studios?

    a. Tell him there is   c. Tell him there is a

       a circus   clown convention

    b. Tell him there is   d. Tell him there is

       a birthday party   a movie

769. Which of these is *not* one of the mind areas Bing Bong points out to Joy and Sadness as they travel on the train of thought?

    a. Mental blocks   c. Deductive

    b. Déjà vu   reasoning

                     d. Language

                     processing

770. Which island collapses into the tracks for the train of thought?

    a. Hockey island   c. Family island

    b. Honesty island   d. Goofball island

771. What are Bing Bong's last words to Joy just before he fades away?
    a. Tell Riley I love her
    b. Good luck Joy
    c. Take her to the moon for me, ok?
    d. Who's the friend who likes to play?

772. Who does Joy employ to help her get back to headquarters?
    a. Mind police
    b. Perfect boyfriend
    c. Jangles
    d. Rainbow unicorn

773. What object does Anger through at the glass to attempt to let Joy and Sadness into headquarters?
    a. A chair
    b. A binder
    c. Fear
    d. A memory

774. Which emotion stops Riley from running away from home?
    a. Fear
    b. Joy
    c. Sadness
    d. Anger

775. When the emotions are looking out over the new areas of Riley's brain, which one does Fear say he hopes it is just a phase?
    a. Friendship island
    b. Fashion island
    c. Tragic vampire romance island
    d. Boy band island

776. Where is Riley's teacher going for summer vacation according to her emotions?
    a. Bermuda
    b. The Bahamas
    c. Brazil
    d. Buenos Aires

777. During the credits, which of the cat's emotions is running the board in headquarters?
    a. Anger
    b. Fear
    c. Joy
    d. Disgust

The Good Dinosaur

778. How do the dinosaurs chop the trees down on their farm?
    - a. Use their tails
    - b. Bite them
    - c. Use an ax
    - d. Run into them with their heads

779. What do the dinosaurs use to water their crops on the farm?
    - a. Bucket
    - b. Mouth
    - c. Cart
    - d. Baskets

780. Which of these is *not* one of the names of the baby dinosaurs?
    - a. Libby
    - b. Buck
    - c. Arlo
    - d. Tammy

781. What animal chases Arlo out of the coop when he is feeding the animals?
    a. Sheep
    b. Cow
    c. Pig
    d. Chicken

Did you know?

Among the twigs that make up the coop, the number A113 can be seen on the left side of the opening when Arlo runs away from the coop.

782. When the mom and dad dinosaurs put their marks on the silo, what substance do they use?
    a. Sap
    b. Mud
    c. Berry juice
    d. Coal

783. What does Arlo call the chickens when he is determined to stop being afraid of them?
    a. Feather brains
    b. Chirpers
    c. Cluckers
    d. Dirt scratchers

784. What sort of bug lands on Arlo's nose when he is walking through the meadow with his dad?
    a. Firefly
    b. Fly
    c. Butterfly
    d. Dragonfly

785. What is the new job Arlo's dad gives him?
    a. Smash the pumpkins
    b. Fill the silo with food for winter
    c. Catch the critter that eats their food
    d. Protect the family from bugs

786. What does Arlo hold in his mouth as a weapon against the critter?
    a. A rock
    b. Wooden log
    c. A hammer
    d. An ax

787. When Arlo and his dad search for the critter, how does Arlo's dad tell him he can find the way home?
    a. Find the river
    b. Find the mountains
    c. Make a trail
    d. Follow his footsteps

788. How does Arlo hurt his leg while tracking the critter?
    a. Tripped over a rock
    b. A tree fell on it
    c. Falls off the rocks
    d. Tripped on a tree root

789. During the harvest, what event is coming that they need to finish before?
    a. The hurricanes
    b. The floods
    c. The first snow
    d. The tornados

> *Did you know?*
>
> When Arlo is floating down the river, he sinks to the bottom of the riverbed. You can see Hank, the octopus from *Finding Dory*, on the left side of the boulder Arlo floats by.

790. When Arlo finds the human after his ride down the rapids, what does the human wear as a skirt?
   a. Bushes
   b. Bark
   c. Flowers
   d. Leaves

791. How does Arlo remove his foot from between the rocks after he falls from the tree?
   a. A wooly mammoth lifts the rocks
   b. The rocks slide down the hill
   c. The human digs him out
   d. He wiggles his leg through the opening

792. What is the first item the human brings to Arlo as an offering?
   a. A fish
   b. A lizard
   c. A giant bug
   d. A turkey

793. What falls out of the tree when Arlo tries to eat the berries?
   a. A scorpion
   b. A snake
   c. A bat
   d. A vulture

Did you know?

The pet collector can be seen in the Pixar film Inside Out in one of the memory orbs when the family takes pictures with the dinosaurs on the road to their new home.

794. When Arlo meets the pet collector, he introduces the animals on his horns. What does the destructor protect him from?
    a. Nothing
    b. Creatures that crawl in the night
    c. Having unrealistic goals
    d. Mosquitos

795. Which of these is *not* one of the names the pet collector thinks up for the human?
    a. Beast
    b. Hemorrhoid
    c. Annihilator
    d. Funeral planner

796. Which of the pet collectors' friends tries to attack Arlo to keep the human for themselves?
    a. Dream crusher
    b. Destructor
    c. Fury
    d. Debbie

797. What does Arlo name the human when competing with the pet collector?
    a. Fido
    b. Spot
    c. Timmy
    d. Mickey

Did you know?

After Arlo and the human eat the fermented berries, Arlo sprouts for more eyes. This looks conspicuously like the character Squishy in the Pixar film Monsters University.

> *Did you know?*
>
> The Luxo Jr. ball can be seen floating by Arlo and the human after eating the fermented berries.

798. What objects does Arlo use to simulate his family to communicate with the human?

    a. Leaves   c. Twigs

    b. Rocks   d. Prairie dogs

799. What sort of dinosaurs save Arlo and Spot from the pterodactyls?

    a. T rex   c. Titanosaurus

    b. Stegosaurus   d. Spinosaurus

> *Did you know?*
>
> The Tyrannosaurus Rex run as if they are riding horses. Notice how they gallop instead of run.

800. What breed of dinosaurs do the T Rex refer to as rustlers?

    a. Velociraptors   c. Spinosaurus

    b. Stegosaurus   d. Allosaurus

> *Did you know?*
>
> The rustlers have feathers that reference the film *Jurassic Park* in which Dr. Grant has a theory in which the dinosaurs all changed into birds.

> **Did you know?**
>
> As the dinosaurs are fighting over the herd, this scene is inspired by the finale of the film *Jurassic Park*.

801. What does the T Rex use as a harmonica when they are around the campfire?
    - a. A tooth
    - b. A twig
    - c. A bone
    - d. A bug

> **Did you know?**
>
> When the dinosaurs compare their scars, this references the film *Jaws* in the scene where the shark hunters are comparing old scars.

> **Did you know?**
>
> The T Rex references the film 127 hours, in which the main character gets his arm stuck between a boulder and a rock wall. She talks about being stuck between a rock and a hard place which is the title of the book by Aron Rolston.

> **Did you know?**
>
> The Pterodactyl wings coming through the cloud are reminiscent of the shark fin in the film *Jaws*.

802. How does Arlo know his dad is not actually with him when he sees his dad in the rainstorm?
    a. He does not talk
    b. He does not have footprints
    c. He walks through him
    d. He cannot speak to him

803. How does Arlo and Spot park from each other?
    a. The Pterodactyls take Spot
    b. Spot gets lost in the rapids
    c. Arlo's family tells him to go
    d. Spot finds his family

Finding Dory

Did you know?

The animators created a receding hairline on Dory's father, a huge accomplishment for an aquatic character.

804. When baby Dory and her parents are playing hide and seek, what does Dory get distracted by while counting?
    a. Coral
    b. Sand
    c. A fish
    d. A seashell

805. What do Dory's parents tell her to be careful of in the ocean?
    a. Undertow
    b. Predators
    c. Seaweed
    d. Red tide

806. What objects are on the ocean floor when Dory meets the crabs?
    a. Cans
    b. Bottles
    c. Computer monitors
    d. Car parts

807. As Dory talks in her sleep, she tells Claus what object is drooping?
    a. Flowers
    b. Chandelier
    c. Curtains
    d. Pinata

808. Where is the field trip going that Mr. Ray is taking the class?
    a. Turtle migration
    b. Stingray migration
    c. Jellyfish migration
    d. Moonfish migration

809. How do the Stingrays know where to go, according to Mr. Ray?
    a. Instinct
    b. Telepathy
    c. Internal maps
    d. They follow each other

810. Finish the name of the institute that Dory remembers after the stingray migration, "The _____ of Morrow Bay California."
    a. Charm
    b. Gem
    c. Jewel
    d. Ocean

811. Who does Marlin know that can help them get across the ocean?
    a. Crush
    b. Squirt
    c. Bruce
    d. Moonfish

812. What is the name of Dory's father?
    a. Cedric
    b. Carl
    c. Cecil
    d. Charlie

> *Did you know?*
>
> The Pizza Planet truck is among the ocean floor objects as Dory, Marlin, and Nemo look for Dory's parents.

813. What does Marlin promise the giant squid if he lets them live?
    a. They will feed him
    b. They will worship him
    c. They will never come back
    d. They will tell others about him

814. What does Dory get caught in while trying to save Nemo, the giant squid?
    a. Fishing line
    b. Fishing net
    c. Seaweed
    d. Six-pack rings

> *Did you know?*
>
> Sigourney Weaver is the voice of the institute,; she also voices the Axiom in the movie *WALL-E*.

> *Did you know?*
>
> The boat that captures Dory has the numbers 1200 and 86 stamped on the edge. This is a reference to the address of Pixar 1200 Park Ave, Emeryville, Ca. The 86 is a reference to 1986, the year Pixar began as a company.

815. Which of these numbers is the correct number on Dory's tag?
    - a. 8131
    - b. 1318
    - c. 3181
    - d. 3118

> *Did you know?*
>
> There is a picture of Darla on the wall behind the tank Dory is placed in quarantine. Darla is the niece of the dentist in *Finding Nemo.*

816. Where do the fish get transported to when they cannot cut it at the institute?
    - a. Cleveland
    - b. Portland
    - c. Oakland
    - d. Richlands

817. What does Hank the octopus drink while talking to Dory in quarantine?
    - a. Water
    - b. Coffee
    - c. Soda
    - d. Milk

818. What is the sea lion's favorite dream when he accuses Marlin and Nemo of disturbing him?
    a. Laying on the rock
    b. Eating fish
    c. Floating
    d. Counting seagulls

Did you know?

The tags on Fluke and Rudder combine to create the number A113. This is the classroom number at Cal Arts, where many of the animators went to school.

Did you know?

There are two hidden Mickey's on the rock formed by the holes in the formation.

819. What is the name of the sea lion Fluke and Rudder chase off the rock they are laying on?
    a. Gerald
    b. George
    c. Gil
    d. Gerard

820. When Hank and Dory look at the map, what does Hank camouflage himself as when the office worker looks out in the hallway?
    a. A coffee pot
    b. A tree
    c. A cabinet
    d. A planter

821. What object do Dory's parents line up so Dory can find her way home as a baby?
    a. Hermit crabs
    b. Pebbles
    c. Shells
    d. Sea glass

Did you know?

As Hank and Dory make their way through the passageway, there is a pipe with the label Seawater Supply DL59. This is a reference to the submarine ride at Disneyland, which began daily operation in 1959. There is an identical pipe in the loading area for this attraction.

---

822. What sea creature is Destiny?
    a. Beluga whale
    b. Whale shark
    c. Octopus
    d. Blue tang

823. How did Dory and Destiny communicate when Dory lived at the institute?
    a. Writing on their tags
    b. Through the enclosures
    c. Passing messages to other sea creatures
    d. The pipes

824. What is the name of the bird that helps Marlin and Nemo get into the institute?
    a. Becky
    b. Brookie
    c. Bailey
    d. Jessica

> *Did you know?*
>
> Several characters from other Pixar films are visitors to the marine institute. Included are children from the Day Care in *Toy Story 3*, teenagers from *Inside Out*, and the dentist-patient from *Finding Nemo*.

825. How do Hank and Dory travel across the institute?
    a. Baby stroller
    b. Wheelchair
    c. Wagon
    d. Walk

826. How many hearts does Dory tell Hank octopus have?
    a. One
    b. Two
    c. Three
    d. Seven

827. When Dory and Hank fall into the touch pool at the Kids Zone, what does the sea cucumber buried in the sand say to Dory?
    a. Touch
    b. Hands
    c. Hello
    d. Beware

828. What happens when Hank gets poked in the face while in the touch pool?
    a. He bites the child
    b. He screams
    c. He jumps out of the pool
    d. He inks

> *Did you know?*
>
> The clam tells Marlin and Nemo how happy he is to see them, a reference to "Happy as a clam."

829. As Dory remembers her parents, what event causes her to get swept away in the undertow?
- a. Trying to get to the ocean
- b. Trying to go to school
- c. Trying to get a purple shell for her mom
- d. Trying to follow her friends

830. Which of these are the correct directions to get Dory back to quarantine?
- a. Two rights and a left
- b. Two lefts and a right
- c. Three lefts and two rights
- d. A left and two rights

831. How is Bailey able to see the quarantine area from her enclosure?
- a. Mental telepathy
- b. Echolocation
- c. X-ray vision
- d. She broke out of her enclosure

Did you know?

As Hank and Dory make their way through the passageway, there is a pipe with the label Seawater Supply DL59. This is a reference to the submarine ride at Disneyland, which began daily operation in 1959. There is an identical pipe in the loading area for this attraction.

832. After Dory is carried through the sewer into the ocean, she is alone and says to herself, " _____ is what I do best."
    a. Forgetting
    b. Messing up
    c. Swimming
    d. Getting lost

833. What nickname does Dory's dad call her when they are reunited?
    a. Little blue
    b. Squishy face
    c. Cupcake
    d. Funny face

834. When Destiny and Bailey attempt to jump over the wall of the institute, what does Bailey offer Destiny to help her?
    a. Her encouragement
    b. Her fin
    c. Her echolocation
    d. Her eyes

835. Which creatures help Dory stop traffic so she can catch up to the truck with Marlin and Nemo aboard?
    a. Octopi
    b. Whales
    c. Sea otters
    d. Sea lions

Did you know?

The Pizza Planet truck is in traffic when the truck is on the highway towards Cleveland.

836. Who saves Dory, Marlin, and Nemo from the truck
     to get them back to the ocean?
     a. Hank   c. Destiny
     b. Becky   d. Bailey

Did you know?

The license plate on the truck transporting the fish reads CALA113. This is another reference to the Cal Arts classroom where the Pixar animators went to school.

Did you know?

The passenger in the transport truck is voiced by Nolan Gould, the original voice of Nemo in *Finding Nemo*. A new actor was brought in to voice the adolescent fish, but the Pixar team wanted to include Gould in the film.

Did you know?

The center of the steering wheel on the truck resembles the Luxo Jr. ball, including the stripe and the star.

837. How does Dory figure out which way the ocean is
     while Hank is driving the truck?
     a. She sees water   c. Seagulls
     b. The beach   d. She remembers
                                   the way

838. What famous song is playing when the truck flies off the cliff into the ocean?
    a. *What a Wonderful World*
    b. *Beyond the Sea*
    c. *The Girl from Ipanema*
    d. *Unforgettable*

839. What job does Hank take after he goes to the ocean?
    a. Real estate agent
    b. Babysitter
    c. Substitute teacher
    d. Police officer

Did you know?

During the credits, Hank appears in camouflage all over the institute. Keep a close eye out for him throughout the scenes.

Did you know?

Be sure to watch the film after the credits finish; there is a scene with the sea lions and the tank gang from *Finding Nemo*.

Cars 3

840. Who does Lightning McQueen dedicate his race to before the Piston Cup?
    a. Cruz Ramirez
    b. Mater
    c. Sally Carrera
    d. Doc Hudson

841. What is Lightning McQueen's speed according to the radar speed sign in ornament valley?
    a. 169
    b. 196
    c. 139
    d. 193

842. What is the first name of the statistical analysis that Chick interviews about the race?
    a. Nellie
    b. Sally
    c. Natalie
    d. Samantha

843. Which of these is *not* one of the areas listed on the display when the statistical analyst explains why Jackson Storm won the race?
    a. Wind resistance
    b. Force
    c. Aero
    d. Racers

> *Did you know?*
>
> As the talk show discusses the races, you will see clips of the race cars on the track. The words BNL can be seen on the inside of the track. This is a reference to the film *WALL-E* in which the global conglomerate Buy N Large is the only shopping option in the future.

844. Which sponsor does # 42 Cal Weathers drive for when he announces his retirement?
     - a. Tow Car
     - b. Apple
     - c. Combusta
     - d. Dinoco

845. What is the name of the newspaper with the headline "CRASH! Hudson Hornet out for season" on the wall of Lightning McQueen's garage?
     - a. The Radiator Springs Times
     - b. The Daily Exhaust
     - c. The Ornament Valley Tribune
     - d. The Daily Dinoco

> *Did you know?*
>
> Filmore's license plate is George Carlin's birthday, the actor who voiced Filmore in the first *Cars* film.

846. What famous landmark does Ramone compare Lightning McQueen to after he finishes painting him?
     - a. The Last Supper
     - b. The Mona Lisa
     - c. The Sistine Chapel
     - d. The Vatican

847. Where does Lizzie tell Lightning McQueen to kick the other racers?
    - a. Trunk
    - b. Hood
    - c. Headlights
    - d. Tires

Did you know?

The Rusteze Racing Center building is in the shape of a stadium.

848. Which of these is *not* one of the jars of dirt that displays the dirt from the racetracks Doc Hudson raced on?
    - a. Los Angeles Motor Speedway
    - b. Florida International Speedway
    - c. Thunder Hollow
    - d. Fireball Beach

849. What is Cruz Ramirez's job at the Rusteze Racing Center?
    - a. Racer
    - b. Trainer
    - c. Technical advisor
    - d. Engineer

Did you know?

The village of Santa Cecilia is shown on the monitor about the treadmills at the racing center. This is a hint to the next Pixar film, *Coco*, that would be released after *Cars 3*.

850. How many times does Lightning hit the wall on his first time on the simulator?
   a. Two
   b. Five
   c. Ten
   d. Four

851. What object does Lightning McQueen destroy while in the simulator?
   a. Souvenir stand
   b. Bathroom
   c. Drinking fountain
   d. Photobooth

852. What sort of vehicle does the simulator tell Lightning McQueen he has disabled after he jumps the barrier?
   a. Firetruck
   b. Ambulance
   c. Police car
   d. Tow truck

Did you know?

CEO Sterling's office number is A113, a reference to the Cal Arts classroom where some Pixar animators went to school to learn animation.

Did you know?

On the shelf behind Sterling is a small pumpkin coach from the film *Cinderella*.

853. When Cruz tells Lightning he is brittle, what does she compare him to?

    a. A board
    c. A piece of chalk
    b. A twig
    d. A fossil

Did you know?

The training equipment Cruz brings to the beach creates the Apple boot-up sound when she turns it on.

854. What is the name of Cruz's electronic personal assistant?

    a. Hamilton
    c. Washington
    b. Jefferson
    d. Thompson

855. What sea creature does Cruz stop for on the beach while training with Lightning?

    a. Lobster
    c. Crab
    b. Turtle
    d. Dolphin

Did you know?

Mac disguises himself as Jocko Flock's Party Supplies. This is a reference to 1950's racer Tim Flock who had a monkey by that name as his co-driver.

856. What is rule number three at Crazy Eights?

    a. No cursing
    c. The last car standing wins
    b. No escape
    d. No kids on the track

> *Did you know?*
>
> The Luxo Jr. ball can be seen on the hood of one of the racers at Crazy Eights.

857. What sort of car is number 42 in the Crazy Eights race?
    a. School bus
    b. Taxicab
    c. RV
    d. Ambulance

> *Did you know?*
>
> The Pizza Planet truck can be seen during the Crazy Eights race. He is hit and flies through the air. You can see the Pizza Planet rocket fly off into the crowd.

858. What does Fritter collect from the cars she destroys?
    a. License plates
    b. Hub caps
    c. Headlights
    d. Rearview mirrors

> *Did you know?*
>
> Mater can be heard singing the song from the Humphrey the Bear cartoon *In the Bag*.

859. What is the name of Mater's cousin that taught him to sing and whistle at the same time?
    a. Lefty
    b. Timmy
    c. Tom
    d. Doyle

> *Did you know?*
>
> When Lightning McQueen and Cruz Ramirez enter the bar, the white guitar from the movie *Coco* can be seen while the band is playing.

860. What does Guido throw off the truck at Lightning to test his reflexes?
    a. Barrels
    b. Rocks
    c. Hay bails
    d. Logs

> *Did you know?*
>
> As Mac travels to Florida, you can catch a glimpse of the SleepWell Motel. This is a reference to the Pixar special *Toy Story of Terror*.

> *Did you know?*
>
> The best drivers in NASCAR are the voices of the other competitors Lightning McQueen races against.

861. How many cars are competing in the Florida 500?
    a. Fifty-five
    b. Forty-three
    c. Fifty-three
    d. Forty-four

> *Did you know?*
>
> The light blue car racing in Florida is the Tripledent Gum team. This is a reference to the movie *Inside Out*.

862. What is Cruz Ramirez's number after she wins the Florida 500?
    a. 99   c. 15
    b. 95   d. 51

863. During the credits, which resident of Radiator Springs can be found in the treadmill room at the Rusteze Racing Center?
    a. Mater   c. Filmore
    b. Lizzie   d. Sally

864. After the credits, you can hear Mater singing about a date with what sort of vehicle?
    a. School bus   c. Clown car
    b. Ice cream truck   d. VW Thing

Coco

865. What holiday is being celebrated at the cemetery?
    a. Día De Los
       Muertos
    b. Halloween
    c. Christmas
    d. Easter

866. As the story of Miguel's family is being told with the multi-colored flags, what color is the flag that depicts the hammering of the nail into the shoe heel?
    a. Orange
    b. Purple
    c. Blue
    d. Green

867. Which of these is *not* one of the professions Miguel says his great-great-grandmother could have gone into instead of making shoes?
    a. Making sparkly underwear for wrestlers
    b. Making fireworks
    c. Making candy
    d. Making pottery

868. What name does Mama Coco call Miguel when he kisses her cheek?
    a. Esteban
    b. Miguel
    c. Julio
    d. Efren

869. How many Tamales does Miguel's grandmother put on his place as the family eats together?
    a. Six
    b. Five
    c. Ten
    d. Two

Did you know?

The Pizza Planet truck drives by Miguel's house as he looks out the window. The sign on the passenger door reads Pizza Planeta.

870. In what year was the family shoe business started according to the sign painted on the building?
    a. 1913
    b. 1912
    c. 1931
    d. 1921

Did you know?

Miguel stops at a stand selling Alebrijes. There is a small figure of Nemo and Marlin on this table.

Did you know?

As the camera pans out to show the village, you will see a stand selling Pinatas in the shape of Woody and Buzz from *Toy Story* and Mike from *Monsters Inc.*

871. What is the name of the dog Miguel finds in the trash can as he goes to work?

    a. Dante   c. Dino

    b. Juan   d. Enrique

Did you know?

On the front of the third album cover for De La Cruz, the number A113 appears in the lower-left corner. This is a reference to the classroom at Cal Arts, where many of the Pixar animators learned the art of animation.

872. What does Miguel's abuelita hit the mariachi with when she catches Miguel with a guitar?

    a. A wooden spoon   c. Her sandal

    b. A broom   d. A shovel

873. Which of Miguel's ancestors make wingtip shoes according to his family?
     a. Papa Julio
     b. Tia Victoria
     c. Tio Franco
     d. Tio Berto

874. What does Dante eat when he jumps on the family ofrenda?
     a. Pan dulce
     b. Corn on the cob
     c. Mole
     d. Oranges

875. After Miguel's guitar is smashed by his abuelita, what does she tell him will make him feel better?
     a. Going to the cemetery
     b. Sleeping
     c. Making shoes
     d. Eating

876. Where does Miguel go to find a guitar so he can play in the plaza?
     a. The crypt of Ernesto De La Cruz
     b. A music store
     c. A friend's house
     d. The Mariachi museum

877. How does Miguel figure out he no longer has a solid body?
     a. He tries to talk to his family
     b. He cannot pick up anything
     c. He cannot see his reflection
     d. Someone walks through him

878. How do the dead come back to earth on Día De Los Muertos?
    a. The bone bridge
    b. The marigold bridge
    c. Up through the ground
    d. The float down from the sky

Did you know?

As Miguel first sees the village of the afterlife, there are skulls prominent through the structures. Skulls can be seen in the empty spaces between also.

---

879. What does the term Alebrijes mean?
    a. Angel creatures
    b. Colorful creatures
    c. Spirit creatures
    d. Godly creatures

880. When Miguel reaches the afterlife gateway, what word is seen at the top of the arch on the building?
    a. Bienvenidos
    b. Entrada
    c. La vida de ultratumba
    d. Adios

881. What does the first man in the life to reentry bring back for his family?
    a. Wine
    b. Flan
    c. Pan dulce
    d. Churros

882. What happens to Hector when he tries to cross the marigold bridge without a photo?
    a. He falls apart
    b. He sinks into the petals
    c. He freezes
    d. The bridge disappears

883. What does Miguel's uncle say he misses when looking into Miguel's face?
    a. His ears
    b. His tongue
    c. His nose
    d. His skin

Did you know?

When the family arrives at the Department of Family Reunions, the number on the door is A113. This classroom at Cal Arts where many of the Pixar animators went to school.

884. What does Mama Imelda call the computer on the desk when she cannot cross over?
    a. Stupid
    b. Devil box
    c. Worthless
    d. Future box

885. What food does Dante steal off the desk at the Department of Family Reunions?
    a. Pan dulce
    b. Churros
    c. Chicken
    d. Sandwich

886. How long does the family have to get a blessing to reverse the curse?
   - a. One day
   - b. Midnight
   - c. Three days
   - d. Sunrise

887. How does Imelda figure out how to find Miguel?
   - a. His scent
   - b. The police
   - c. Her Alebrije
   - d. They follow Dante

888. What does Hector use to paint Miguel's face to blend in?
   - a. Coal dust
   - b. Paint
   - c. Shoe polish
   - d. Chalk

Did you know

As the monkey and Dante run around the building, the Luxo Jr. ball can be seen on one of the desks in the background.

Did you know?

Miguel runs into Frida Kahlo as he explores the building looking for Ernesto De La Cruz.

889. What did Hector eat when he was poisoned?
   - a. Menudo
   - b. Chorizo
   - c. Mole
   - d. Tacos

890. What happens to the dead when they are not remembered on Día De Los Muertos?
    a. They fade
    b. They turn to dust
    c. They forget their family
    d. They are cursed

> *Did you know?*
>
> As you see the group of people at Plaza De La Cruz that lights the firework ring, there is a poster of *The Incredibles* on the wall of the building to the right.

> *Did you know?*
>
> One of the musicians is wearing the skull T-shirt Sid wears in the original *Toy Story* movie.

891. What instruments do the three nuns play during the contest?
    a. Trumpets
    b. Tubas
    c. Accordions
    d. Xylophones

892. Where do the mariachi's hide Miguel when they enter the tram to Ernesto's tower party?
    a. Sousaphone
    b. Drum
    c. Bass
    d. Xylophone

893. Which abrijes is serving cocktail hot dogs at Ernesto's party?
    a. Turtle
    c. Porcupine
    b. Bird
    d. Rabbit

894. How does Miguel get Ernesto De La Cruz's attention at the party?
    a. He screams
    c. He Dances
    b. He sings
    d. He jumps in the pool

895. What sport is being played at Ernesto's party while he introduces his great-great-grandson?
    a. Soccer
    c. Polo
    b. Horse racing
    d. Jousting

896. What animal is the alebrijes sleeping in Ernesto's arms as he gives Miguel a tour of his home?
    a. Rabbit
    c. Lamb
    b. Burro
    d. Chihuahua

897. How does Ernesto kill Hector?
    a. Shot
    c. Poison his drink
    b. Stabbed
    d. Hit him in the head

898. What does Ernesto tell Miguel does not come for free?
    a. Success
    c. Fame
    b. Blessings
    d. Reputation

899. Why did Hector want to cross the bridge so badly?
    a. To see his daughter
    b. To be remembered
    c. To bring back offerings
    d. To see Miguel

900. Who saves Miguel from the sinkhole he and Hector are thrown into?
    a. Ernesto
    b. Coco
    c. Imelda
    d. Frida

901. What does Imelda hit Ernesto with when they find him backstage?
    a. A guitar
    b. Her shoe
    c. Her arm
    d. A tuba

902. When Miguel returns to the land of the living, where does he return?
    a. The village square
    b. Imelda's grave
    c. His home
    d. Ernesto's crypt

903. How does Miguel help Mama Coco remember Hector?
    a. He gives her Hector's picture
    b. He shows her his picture
    c. He sings to her
    d. The ancestors visit her

904. What did Mama Coco keep to remember her father in her drawer?
    a. His letters
    b. His wedding ring
    c. His notebook
    d. Her baby picture

Did you know?

During the credits, the animators created an ofrenda for all Pixar film's contributors who passed away through the years.

The Incredibles 2

905. Which of these is the correct film number?
    a. File 72-812
    b. File 71-822
    c. File 81-712
    d. File 82-712

906. How does Tony learn Violet is a superhero?
    a. She tells him
    b. She takes her mask off
    c. He sees her costume
    d. He sees Dash as a superhero

907. What is the mascot of Violet's school painted on the side of the building?
   a. Dolphins
   b. Tritons
   c. Romans
   d. Spartans

908. Which superhero saves the monorail from crashing while trying to stop the Underminers drill?
   a. Elastigirl
   b. Mr. Incredible
   c. Frozone
   d. Dash

909. What building is the Underminers drill headed for in the city?
   a. The hospital
   b. The bank
   c. City Hall
   d. The orphanage

910. What does the police tell the Incredibles they would have preferred they do?
   a. Save the city
   b. Catch the Underminer
   c. Save the bank
   d. Nothing

911. What is the name of the motel the Incredibles arrive at after being released from the police?
   a. Safari Court
   b. Safari Motel
   c. Disneyland Hotel
   d. Cozy Cone Motel

912. What movie is on the television when Dash turns it on at the motel?
   a. King Kong
   b. Godzilla
   c. Jaws
   d. Them!

> **Did you know?**
>
> Usher makes a cameo as the limo driver.

913. What is Winston Deavor's official title with Devtech?
    - a. Chief operations officer
    - b. Chief Financial officer
    - c. Chief executive officer
    - d. Chief petty officer

> **Did you know?**
>
> The address for Devtech is 1200 Park Ave; this is the street address for Pixar Animation Studio in Emeryville, Ca. The area code for the phone number is the correct area code for Emeryville also.

914. Which superhero statue did Winston's father donate money to construct?
    - a. Dynaguy
    - b. Syndrome
    - c. Gazerbeam
    - d. Fironic

915. What is Evelyn's job at Devtech?
    - a. Security officer
    - b. Telecommunications
    - c. I.T.
    - d. Designer

916. What reason does Mr. Incredible give for superheroes being forced underground?
    - a. Perception
    - b. Ignorance
    - c. Evil
    - d. Politics

917. What sort of ball is Winston playing with while he is on the phone with Elastigirl?
   a. Football
   b. Basketball
   c. Baseball
   d. Soccer ball

918. Which piece of fruit does Mr. Incredible eat out of the fruit basket first?
   a. Orange
   b. Apple
   c. Pear
   d. Grapes

919. What color is the pacifier that Jack-Jack has while Mr. Incredible is holding him?
   a. Blue
   b. Red
   c. Green
   d. Yellow

920. When Elastigirl finds the new motorcycle in the garage, what secret about herself does she share with Mr. Incredible?
   a. She was a blonde
   b. She had green hair
   c. She shaved her head
   d. She had a mohawk

921. What is the name of the breakfast cereal Dash tries to pour for breakfast?
   a. Sugar Flakes
   b. Sugar Bombs
   c. Frosted Bombs
   d. Frosted Nuggets

922. What is the name of the book Mr. Incredible reads to Jack-Jack at bedtime?
    a. Moozles Mornings
    b. Woozles Waking
    c. Choozles Chores
    d. Doozles Dozing

Did you know?

The Incredibles 2 is based on the 1960s television shows; architecture and vehicles reflect this era.

923. What is the name of the building behind Elastigirl while watches the ribbon cutting of the hovertrain?
    a. Examiner
    b. Times
    c. Chronicle
    d. Tribune

924. What is Dash looking for when he calls Elastigirl while she chases the train?
    a. His math book
    b. His high tops
    c. His backpack
    d. His super suit

925. In what year was the tunnel established that Elastigirl ducks under while on the top of the train?
    a. 1954
    b. 1964
    c. 1924
    d. 1944

926. What sort of animal is on the side of Jack Jack's crib when Mr. Incredible puts him to sleep?
    a. Seal
    b. Swan
    c. Puppy
    d. Lion

> *Did you know?*
>
> The Luxo Jr. ball can be found on the design in Jack Jack's crib.

> *Did you know?*
>
> There is a figure of Duke Kaboom on the mobile attached to Jack Jack's crib. This is a reference to *Toy Story 4*, the next film in the Pixar movies.

927. What sort of animal does Jack-Jack find eating out of the garbage while watching television?
   a. Bead
   b. Racoon
   c. Opossum
   d. Coyote

928. Which of these is *not* one of the powers Jack-Jack displays while fighting the animal in the yard?
   a. Transfiguration
   b. Laser vision
   c. Spontaneous combustion
   d. Multiplying

929. What is the time when Mr. Incredible goes to bed after speaking with Elastigirl on the phone?
   a. 2:17
   b. 7:12
   c. 3:10
   d. 8:14

930. Where did Violet write her address so Tony would not forget to take her out?
    a. On his hand
    b. On his binder
    c. On his locker
    d. On his forehead

Did you know?

Elastigirl has a brief conversation with Ambassador Henrietta Selick before her interview; she later saves the Ambassador's life. This is a tribute to animator/director Henry Selick, famous for the stop motion animation *James and the Giant Peach*, *Coraline*, and *The Nightmare Before Christmas*.

931. What is the television station Elastigirl does the interview with Chad?
    a. KTTV
    b. KQRY
    c. KWED
    d. KPXR

932. How many pages does the New Urbem Times Elastigirl is reading contain with the headline, "Elastigirl Saves Ambassador."?
    a. Two hundred ninety-two
    b. Ninety-three
    c. Twenty-Nine
    d. Ninety-two

933. What sort of food does Winston have in his hand while Elastigirl meets the new superheroes?
    a. Brownie
    b. Apple
    c. Cookie
    d. Slice of cake

934. As the family arrives at The Happy Platter, Mr. Incredible asks for a booth new what sort of flowers?

    a. Chrysanthemums
    b. Philodendrons
    c. Hibiscus
    d. Rhododendron

Did you know?

As Elastigirl explores the building where the Screen Slaver's signal came from, she hears a grandfather clock chime. The design on the back of the clock is a hidden Mickey.

Did you know?

In the scene when Jack-Jack disappears into another dimension while chewing on the television remote, this is a reference to the 1982 film *Poltergeist*.

935. What is the name of the 1960s cartoon Dash watches while Mr. Incredible is sleeping on the couch?

    a. The Super Friends
    b. Speed Racer
    c. Johnny Quest
    d. Batman and Robin

936. Which classical composer does Edna use to demonstrate Jack Jack's superpowers?

    a. Brahms
    b. Mozart
    c. Beethoven
    d. Handel

937. What flavor is the flame retardant built into Jack Jack's super suit?
    a. Blackberry Sage
    b. Blueberry rose
    c. Boysenberry pumpkin spice
    d. Blackberry lavender

938. How much did Edna charge for babysitting Jack-Jack?
    a. Free
    b. Fifty thousand dollars
    c. Seventy-five cents
    d. Twenty-two dollars

939. Who did Elastigirl put in jail when she thought she was fighting The Screen Slaver?
    a. Taco delivery guy
    b. Grocery delivery guy
    c. Uber driver
    d. Pizza delivery guy

Did you know?

The Pizza Planet truck is parked nearby in an alley when Elastigirl lands with the Screen Slaver.

940. What does Jack Jack's family use to get him to come out of the other dimension?
    a. His favorite toy
    b. A pacifier
    c. A cookie
    d. A popsicle

> *Did you know?*
>
> When Evelyn comments that Einstein was a patent clerk, this is a reference to the 1984 film Ghostbusters, in which Dr. Venkman makes this comment to Ray after they are removed from the university.

941. How does Elastigirl get the Screen Slaver goggles on Mr. Incredible?
    - a. Kisses him
    - b. Beats him up
    - c. Ties him up
    - d. Freezes him

942. How do the superheroes find out Violet is on the ship?
    - a. She makes noise
    - b. She forgets to disappear
    - c. She knocks over a plant
    - d. She bumps into a superhero

943. Who pulls the glasses off Elastigirl's face when they arrive on the bridge of the ship?
    - a. Violet
    - b. Jack-Jack
    - c. Dash
    - d. Frozone

944. Which of the new superheroes was missing after the Incredibles removed the goggles from each superhero?
    - a. Krushaur
    - b. Reflux
    - c. Brick
    - d. He-Lectrix

945. What is the name of the school dance that is on the poster near Tony?
    a. Prince and Princess
    b. Under the sea
    c. Enchanted night
    d. Happily ever after

946. What is the name of the movie Violet and Tony see when the family takes them on a date?
    a. *Too Many Supers*
    b. *High Anxiety*
    c. *Dementia 113*
    d. *The Parent Trap*

Did you know?

The movie's name includes A113, the classroom number at Cal Arts, where most of the Pixar animators went to school.

Did you know?

You will hear the superhero themes for Mr. Incredible, Elastigirl, and Frozone during the credits.

Toy Story 4

947. Which toy is left out in the rain when Andy comes into the house with his toys?
   a. RC car
   b. Slinky dog
   c. Rex
   d. Mr. Potato Head

948. Which of these is *not* one of the names of Bo Peep's sheep?
   a. Billy
   b. McGee
   c. Goat
   d. Gruff

949. What is the name of the operation to save the lost toy from the gutter?
   a. Operation jump rope
   b. Operation slinky toy
   c. Operation pull toy
   d. Operation hula hoop

> *Did you know?*
>
> The license plate on the car that comes to the house during the rainstorm reads RMRF97. This references an incident in 1997 when the animators accidentally deleted most of Toy Story 2 with the command rm -r -f. Luckily for the Pixar crew, there was a backup at the house of one of the animators.

950. What character does Bonnie decide Hamm is going to play during playtime?
     a. Ice cream man   c. Sheriff
     b. Mayor   d. Baker

951. Which toy becomes the sheriff when Bonnie takes the star off Woody's chest?
     a. Buzz Lightyear   c. Rex
     b. Jessie   d. Hamm

> *Did you know?*
>
> The closet toys are voiced by veteran actors Mel Brookes, Betty White, and Carl Reiner.

952. Which of these is *not* one of the names the toys in the closet suggest Woody name is first dust bunny?
     a. Roger   c. Karen
     b. Lebron   d. Thumper

953. Which role does Mr. Prickle Pants say he was born to play?
    a. Sheriff   c. Hat shop owner
    b. Baker   d. Ice cream man

954. What is the name of Bonnie's kindergarten teacher?
    a. Miss Maria   c. Miss Lynne
    b. Miss Brooke   d. Miss Wendy

> *Did you know?*
>
> As Bonnie walks over to put her backpack away, a girl with brunette hair is sitting at the table that resembles Boo from *Monsters Inc.*

955. What name is on the yellow cubby to the right of Bonnie's red cubby?
    a. Vivienne   c. Anton
    b. Caleb   d. Mary

956. What does the boy have in his mouth when he takes the art supply box from Bonnie's table?
    a. Lollipop   c. Licorice
    b. Apple   d. Celery

> *Did you know?*
>
> The lunchbox that Woody hides behind in the classroom has Reptillus Maximus on it. This is a reference to the Toy Story That Time Forgot Christmas special.

957. What is Forky's first word to the toys in Bonnie's room?
    a. Woody
    b. Hi
    c. Forky
    d. Trash

958. What is the shape of the sticker on Forky's foot?
    a. Rainbow
    b. Happy face
    c. Star
    d. Unicorn

> *Did you know?*
>
> Bonnie's family stops at Dinoco gas, from the film *Cars* and Poultry Palace from the Pixar short *Small Fry*.

959. What does Bonnie place on Woody's feet while playing at Poultry Palace?
    a. Creamer containers
    b. Ketchup packets
    c. Dipping sauce containers
    d. Sugar packets

960. Which of these is *not* one of the purposes that Forky tells Woody he was made for?
    a. Soup
    b. Pudding
    c. Salad
    d. Chili

961. When Woody asks Hamm how far they have till the next stop, what does Hamm tell him?
    a. 5.32 miles
    b. 5.23 miles
    c. 3.25 miles
    d. 2.35 miles

962. What is the name of Gabby Gabby's ventriloquist doll that pushes her carriage?
   a. Vincent   c. Mortimer
   b. Charlie   d. Boris

963. What is the name of the child Gabby Gabby wants to adopt her?
   a. Melanie   c. Tiffany
   b. Melody   d. Harmony

964. What object does Woody get his foot caught in while running from the ventriloquist doll?
   a. Adding machine   c. Typewriter
   b. Wire cooling rack   d. Cash register

Did you know?

After the shop owner gives Woody to her granddaughter and waves goodbye, you can see a photograph of Geri from the Pixar short Geri's Game on the wall behind her.

965. What do the toys use to replace Forky while Bonnie is sleeping in the RV?
   a. A crayon   c. A marker
   b. A fork   d. A spoon

Did you know?

The carnival worker has a Pizza Planet truck tattoo on the back of his leg when he bends over to pick up Buzz Lightyear.

> *Did you know?*
>
> There is a toy guitar with the same design as Ernesto De La Cruz from the film *Coco* on the game booth wall at the carnival.

966. How many toy guitars are seen in the game booth Buzz is zip tied to at the carnival?
    - a. Seven
    - b. Four
    - c. Five
    - d. Twelve

967. What does Bo Peep use to camouflage herself and woody when they escape from the playground?
    - a. Frisbee
    - b. Kite
    - c. Basketball
    - d. Soccer ball

968. What is the first item the sheep find for Bo Peep while exploring the shrubs around the park?
    - a. Drinking straw
    - b. Paper clip
    - c. Bandage
    - d. Safety pin

> *Did you know?*
>
> The batteries that operates the skunk is Buy N Large, the brand from the film *WALL-E*.

969. What sort of party do Combat Karl and friends crash on another playground?
    - a. Pinata
    - b. Skating
    - c. Pool
    - d. Ice cream

970. What does Chicky call Buzz Lightyear when they are zip-tied to the game booth?
    a. Astro boy
    b. Lunar boy
    c. Space boy
    d. Talking boy

971. What do the sheep use to drive the skunk as they work their way through the carnival?
    a. A screwdriver
    b. Their ears
    c. Their paws
    d. Their tongues

972. Which ride do Bo Peep and Woody climb to the top to work their way back to the antique store?
    a. Bumper cars
    b. Carousel
    c. Ferris wheel
    d. Funhouse

973. What did Jessie use to flatten the tire on the RV?
    a. A screwdriver
    b. A wrench
    c. A nail
    d. Unscrewed the air valve cap

Did you know?

The dogs playing poker painting inside the antique store is a reference to the Pixar film *Up*.

974. What does Bo Peep call the cat that guards the antique store?
    a. Hippopotamus
    b. Crocodile
    c. Rhinoceros
    d. Dragon

> *Did you know?*
>
> As Bonnie and her mother enter the antique store, you can see the scuba mask from *Finding Nemo* and a Casey Jr. lunch box from *A Bugs Life*.

975. What item does Bo Peep knock over to stop Vincent from capturing Woody?
    a. Croquet mallet
    b. Golf club
    c. Broom
    d. Baseball bat

> *Did you know?*
>
> While Woody watches someone shopping from behind the red phone, you can see the Alebrije Dante from the movie *Coco* on one of the shelves.

> *Did you know?*
>
> Woody poses on top of a red phone with the receiver hanging from his arm. This pose is taken directly from the Mickey Mouse phones that were sold in the 1980s.

> *Did you know?*
>
> When the camera angle is shown from behind Woody on the red phone, you will see Riley and Bing Bing's rocket on the left side on one of the shelves.

976. What game does Gabby Gabby tell Forky they will play when they find out Woody and Bo Peep are back?
   a. Tag
   b. House
   c. Go fish
   d. Hide and go seek

977. What sort of coin-operated device does Bo Peep open a secret compartment for herself and Woody to enter?
   a. Vending machine
   b. Pinball machine
   c. Slot machine
   d. Video game

Did you know?

The toy that opens the door for Bo Peep and Woody is Tinny from the Pixar short Tin Toy.

978. What does Bo Peep call Woody to get him in the party with the toys in the hidden compartment?
   a. Her friend
   b. Her moving buddy
   c. Her accessory
   d. Her boyfriend

979. What is the name of the zebra toy that the cat tore in half?
   a. Bob
   b. Mel
   c. George
   d. Doug

980. How many different poses does Duke Kaboom do for Woody while Bo Peep introduces them?
    a. Eleven
    b. Ten
    c. Seven
    d. Five

981. What is the name of the child that received Duke Kaboom for Boxing Day?
    a. Rejean
    b. Benjamin
    c. Christian
    d. Keanu

Did you know?

The stack of game boxes next to the projector on the high shelf all have names from Pixar short cartoons. *Lifted, Knick Knack,* and *Lava* can be read on the boxes.

982. What do the toys use to haul Duke Kaboom's motorcycle launcher up to the high shelf?
    a. Jump rope
    b. 8mm film
    c. Yarn
    d. Christmas garland

Did you know?

As the toys are hauling Duke Kaboom's motorcycle launcher up the shelves, you can see a handkerchief with Wally B from Pixar's first animation, *The Adventures of Andre and Wally B.*

> *Did you know?*
>
> You can see a Grape Soda's sign above the shelf as the woman walks by holding the wooden duck. This is a reference to the grape soda bottle cap from the film *UP*.

983. What product does the sign for Atom Pops advertise in front of Woody and Bo Peep when they move Duke Kaboom's launcher?
     a. Crackers
     b. Lollipops
     c. Popcorn
     d. Cookies

> *Did you know?*
>
> Among the chandeliers in the antique store is a megaphone from *Monsters University* and an airplane from the film *Planes*.

> *Did you know?*
>
> As Giggles McDimple is looking out over the store, you can see the Pizza Planet rocket on the left

984. What does the center of the clock read with the green neon that Giggles McDimple uses to signal Duke Kaboom?
     a. Time for burgers
     b. Time for coffee
     c. Time for Timer
     d. Time for donuts

985. What does Duke Kaboom say to the cat when he lands on the floor?
   a. What's new pussy cat?
   b. Hey fat cat
   c. It's a cat on a hot tin roof
   d. Cat got your tongue

> Did you know?
> As one of the Ventriloquist dolls falls from the high shelf, you will see a square picture hanging with A113 in orange tones. This is a reference to the classroom at Cal Arts, where most of the Pixar animators went to school.

> *Did you know?*
>
> As the toys look down on the shop, you can see the Luxo Jr. ball on the floor to the left side of the screen.

986. Which toy does the cat swallow?
   a. Duke Kaboom
   b. Billy Goat and Gruff
   c. Giggles McDimple
   d. Forky

> *Did you know?*
>
> There is a box to the left side of the screen while the cat chases Duke Kaboom that reads Pixar. Also seen during the chase is a set of drinking glasses with the characters from *WALL-E*.

987. What object does Woody use as a weapon when he runs into Gabby Gabby and her ventriloquist dolls?
   a. Crayon
   b. Pencil
   c. Safety pin
   d. Paper clip

988. What does Woody give up to save Forky from Gabby Gabby?
   a. His child
   b. His freedom
   c. His hat
   d. His voice box

989. Which of Bonnie's toys remind her that she left her backpack at the antique store?
   a. Buzz Lightyear
   b. Jessie
   c. Bullseye
   d. Rex

990. What does the label read on the tin can beneath the carousel at the carnival?
   a. Creamed corn
   b. Pork and beans
   c. Low-fat lard
   d. Spicy chili

991. What items are in the box Harmony throws Gabby Gabby into?
   a. Old tools
   b. Logs
   c. Puzzle pieces
   d. Wooden blocks

992. What does the woman find in the baby carriage that makes her scream?
   a. Skunk
   b. A ventriloquist doll
   c. Chicky and Bunny
   d. Gabby Gabby

993. Which toy is the voice of the GPS in the RV when they are trying to get the family to the carousel?
    a. Buttercup
    b. Mr. Prickle Pants
    c. Trixie
    d. Jessie

> *Did you know?*
>
> One of the carnival games is called Dragon Zone, with a picture of Figment on the booth.

> *Did you know?*
>
> On the side of the bouncy castle is the unicorn painted on the side of the van from the Pixar film *Onward*.

994. What do Ducky and Bunny roll across the lost girl's path to make her look at Gabby Gabby?
    a. Baseball
    b. Ping Pong ball
    c. Skee ball
    d. Plastic ball

995. What is Forky's job when the toys are trying to get back to the RV?
    a. Roll up the windows
    b. Lock the car doors
    c. Activate the awning
    d. Close the RV door

996. What does Woody give to Jessie when he stays
behind with Bo Peep?

    a. His holster   c. Bullseye

    b. His hat   d. His badge

Did you know?

After the credits, there is a tribute to Don Rickles, the
voice of Mr. Potato Head and animator Ada Burke.

Onward

997. As the stove is being demonstrated for the crown, find the sign to the left of the display. What sort of hearths are being sold?
    a. Self-starting
    b. Self-cleaning
    c. Woodless
    d. Gas-powered

998. What is the name of the video game to the right of Prance Prance at the arcade?
    a. Crystal
    b. Gauntlet
    c. Sword of Thunder
    d. Thunder Cats

999. What sort of mythical creature is rummaging through the garbage cans on the street?
    a. Unicorns
    b. Satyrs
    c. Leprechauns
    d. Centaurs

1000. What event takes place on the 8th of the month, according to Ian's calendar?

    a. Football practice

    b. Chess club meeting

    c. Math club meeting

    d. Physics club meeting

1001. What is the name of Ian's pet dragon?

    a. Fireball

    b. Blazer

    c. Pyro

    d. Blazey

1002. According to Barley, how fast could centaurs run in days of yore?

    a. Sixty miles per hour

    b. Seventy miles per hour

    c. One hundred seventy miles per hour

    d. Ninety miles per hour

Did you know?

Laurel uses Aurora brand dish soap. Aurora is a synonym for Dawn.

1003. Which of these is *not* one of the memories Barley has of his father?

    a. He used to play drums on his feet

    b. His beard was scratchy

    c. He had a goofy laugh

    d. He had a big belly

> *Did you know?*
>
> There is a patch on Barley's jacket in the shape of the Infinity Gauntlet, a reference to the Marvel films.

1004. What is Ian's father's first name?
   - a. Willard
   - b. Wilden
   - c. William
   - d. Willem

> *Did you know?*
>
> When Ian goes to the Burger Shire, there is a sign that reads Now Serving 2nd Breakfast. This is a reference to *Lord of the Rings* books.

1005. While Ian is in driving school, and stopped at the corner. What business is being advertised on the yellow sign at the outdoor mall?
   - a. Locksmith
   - b. Psychic
   - c. Car stereo shoppe
   - d. Natural foods

> *Did you know?*
>
> One of the shops in the outdoor mall is called Sword in the Scone, a reference to the Disney film *The Sword in the Stone*.

> *Did you know?*
>
> The calendar pinned to the board in Ian's room has the forest scene from the movie *Brave* on it.

1006. What was Ian's father's job?
    a. Banker
    b. Accountant
    c. Insurance broker
    d. Dentist

1007. What sort of gem is included in the gift Ian's father left for his sons?
    a. Sapphire gem
    b. Dragon gem
    c. Unicorn gem
    d. Phoenix gem

1008. How does Barley let his father's lower half know that he is there?
    a. He taps on his shoe
    b. He touches his leg
    c. He yells into his pants
    d. He holds his ankle

> *Did you know?*
>
> The name of Barley's van is Guinevere. This is a reference to King Arthur's wife and queen in the twelfth century.

1009. What item does Ian try to use the Aloft Evelar spell on inside Barley's van?
    a. Sneaker
    b. Soda can
    c. Old hamburger
    d. CD

> *Did you know?*
>
> The Pizza Planet truck from Toy Story can be seen at the troll toll bridge.

1010. What does Ian use to keep his father walking when they arrive at the tavern?
   - a. Bungee cord
   - b. Rope
   - c. Leash
   - d. Extension cord

> *Did you know?*
>
> The staff at the tavern wear sorcerer hats similar to the hat from The Sorcerer's Apprentice from *Fantasia*.

1011. When Barley asks the Manticore for the map to the stone, what does she give him?
   - a. An atlas
   - b. A children's menu
   - c. A road map
   - d. A coloring book

> *Did you know?*
>
> The Luxo Jr. ball can be seen in one of the shields at the Manticores Tavern.

> *Did you know?*
>
> Remy from the film *Ratatouille* is seen in the background cooking at the Manticore's Tavern.

1012. When Ian and Barley remind the Manticore of who she was, what does she tell the patrons to get them out of the building?
    a. Closed for remodeling
    b. Gas leak
    c. PG13 restaurant now
    d. Closed forever

1013. What is the name of the child that solved the map puzzle for Ian and Barley?
    a. Cathy
    b. Carrie
    c. Kayla
    d. Kendall

1014. What fast food restaurant does Laurel's boyfriend call her from?
    a. Fry Fortress
    b. Burger Battlement
    c. Taco Tower
    d. Chicken Castle

1015. What is the number of the police car that the Manticore sits on while she talks to Laurel?
    a. 1064
    b. 1604
    c. 1460
    d. 1406

1016. What is the name of the pixie gang that enters the convenience store at the gas station?
    a. Pixie Punks
    b. Pixie Dusters
    c. Pixie Riders
    d. Pixie Perils

1017. What does the gas station attendant use as a key chain for the restroom key?
   a. Wooden plank
   b. Hub cap
   c. License plate
   d. Used lotto scratcher

1018. What is the price for a six-pack of Satyrade at the convenience store?
   a. $4.29
   b. $2.49
   c. $9.25
   d. $4.39

Did you know?

There is a display of Tripledent gum at the convenience store. This is a reference to the film *Inside Out*.

1019. Why did the Manticore sell the curse crusher sword?
   a. To pay her mortgage
   b. Tax trouble
   c. Needed a new oven
   d. Paid for her mother's operation

1020. When Ian casts the disguise spell, what is the one thing that will make the spell stop working?
   a. Losing focus
   b. Sweating
   c. Anxiety
   d. Lying

1021. How does the Manticore paralyze the pawnshop owner when she tried to raise the price of her sword?
   a. Vulcan nerve pinch
   b. With the sword
   c. With her scorpion tail
   d. Gave her a paralyzing potion

Did you know?

Barley refers to the gelatinous cube during their quest. This is a reference to Dungeons and Dragons giant cube of Jell-O.

1022. What falls off of Guinevere when Barley sends her on her quest to block the road?
   a. Turn signal
   b. Headlight
   c. Hood ornament
   d. Hub cap

1023. What mythical creatures come out of the darkness at Ian and Barley when they enter the cave to follow the water?
   a. Unicorns
   b. Trolls
   c. Satyrs
   d. Centaurs

1024. When Barley suggests they float down the river using the velocity spell, what do they use as a boat?
   a. Sleeping unicorn
   b. Log
   c. Giant cheese puff
   d. Sleeping troll

1025. What lands on Laurel's windshield, causing her to crash her car?
    a. Fairy
    b. Pixie duster
    c. Flying gnome
    d. Elf

1026. Where do Ian and Barley arrive after they finish the path of peril?
    a. A dead-end
    b. Their house
    c. The Manticore Tavern
    d. Ian's high school

1027. What is the last item on Ian's list of things he wants to do with his father?
    a. Play catch
    b. Share my life with him
    c. Laugh together
    d. Driving lesson

Did you know?

Ian performs a fireworks spell, and one of the fireworks is in the shape of a hidden Mickey.

1028. What does the sign in front of the high school say when the curse tears it from its base?
    a. First day of school
    b. School dance this Friday
    c. Have a great weekend
    d. Remember your permission slips

1029. What shape does the curse take on with the broken pieces of concrete?

    a. Dragon   c. Golem

    b. Minotaur   d. Griffin

1030. Which character stabs the curse to stop it from killing Ian and Barley?

    a. The Manticore   c. Their father

    b. Laurel   d. Colt

Did you know?

When Ian talks with Laurel and Colt, you can hear the voice on Colt's radio saying, "We have an A113 in progress. This is a reference to the classroom at Cal Arts, where most of the Pixar animators attended school.

Soul

1031. In what key is the music on the blackboard in the classroom written?
    a. C natural
    b. B sharp
    c. D flat
    d. D six

1032. What time is shown on the clock in the music classroom?
    a. 3:24
    b. 11:34
    c. 6:52
    d. 10:34

1033. Which of these is *not* one of the perks the principal mentions when she offers Joe a full-time job at the school?
    a. Pension
    b. Summer vacation
    c. Job security
    d. Pension

1034. What sort of store is Libba's?
    a. Shoe repair
    b. Clothing store
    c. Jamaican cuisine
    d. Tailoring and alterations

1035. According to the marquee, what group is playing at the Half Note club?
- a. The Smiles Davis Quintet
- b. The Dorothea Williams Quartet
- c. The World Trombone Quartet
- d. The Count Tracy Orchestra

1036. What is the nickname of Lamont Baker?
- a. Curly
- b. Moe
- c. Tiny
- d. Sticks

1037. As Joe passes by the grocery store, which item advertised on the window is $1.29?
- a. Bananas
- b. Garlic
- c. Tomatoes
- d. Avocado

1038. How old is the soul Joe talks to while riding the escalator to the great beyond?
- a. One hundred seven years old
- b. One hundred six years old
- c. One hundred five years old
- d. One hundred then years old

1039. Finish this line uttered by a soul, "This beats my dream about the _____."
- a. Elephant
- b. Hippopotamus
- c. Walrus
- d. Platypus

1040. Finish this line utter by a soul, "Where are my
_____?"

    a. Pants   c. Glasses

    b. Shoes   d. Gloves

1041. What does the universe use to count the souls going
to the great beyond?

    a. Abacus   c. Adding machine

    b. Calculator   d. Their fingers

1042. What area do the first four souls go to in the great
before?

    a. Earth portal   c. Personality

    b. Aloof   pavilion

                       d. Excitable pavilion

1043. How many souls per minute enter the great beyond,
according to Terry?

    a. 102.5   c. 125

    b. 105.2   d. 152

1044. What is one of the great gifts of the universe?

    a. Remembering   c. Forgetting

        why you were   the trauma of

        born   childbirth

    b. Forgetting   d. Forgetting what

        childhood   life on earth is like

1045. What goes in the missing spot each soul needs to complete their personality?

    a. Zing   c. Flame

    b. Spark   d. Tingle

1046. Which of these is *not* one of the mentor's number twenty-two has had at the institute?

    a. Albert Einstein   c. Abraham Lincoln

    b. Mother Theresa   d. Gandhi

Did you know?

As Joe and number 22 walkthrough his life, a statue is reminiscent of the Partners statue at Disneyland and Walt Disney World's Magic Kingdom. Look for the statue of the adult holding the child's hand. This is the same pose as Walt Disney holding onto the hand of Mickey Mouse.

1047. What item sits on the table in Dr. Borgensonn's office while Joe walks through his memories?

    a. Glass of water   c. Plant

    b. Toy train   d. Toy duck

Did you know?

Number 22 is holding a piece of cake while Marie Antoinette is speaking to her?

1048. What sort of puzzles does number 22 like to do while floating through the mist?
    a. Jigsaw
    b. Crossword
    c. Sudoku
    d. Anagram

1049. What sort of cologne does Joe use on Earth?
    a. Sailor noon
    b. Hugo Brass
    c. Brute
    d. Noir Rouge

Did you know?

When number 22 talks about everything being an illusion, she does an impression of Karl Frederickson from the Pixar film *Up!*

1050. What reason does number 22 give for using the voice she chose?
    a. It sounds like everyone else
    b. It annoys people
    c. She likes it
    d. It makes people stay away

Did you know?

As Joe and number 22 enter the Hall of Everything, the airship from the movie *Up* is in the sky. In the distance, you can also see the outline of the Axiom from *WALL-E*.

> *Did you know?*
>
> The Pizza Planet truck can be found to the left when Joe and number 22 enter the Hall of Everything.

> *Did you know?*
>
> In the Hall of Everything, you will see the hanging Whale from the Pixar film *Finding Dory*.

1051. What sort of camera does the soul use to take a picture of the souls in the rubber raft?
    a. Polaroid   c. Instamatic
    b. Digital   d. Kodak

> *Did you know?*
>
> The Luxo Jr. lamp can be seen in the background when Joe and number 22 are watching the souls.

1052. What sort of ball hits Joe as he and number 22 walk through the Hall of Everything?
    a. Football   c. Soccer ball
    b. Basketball   d. Baseball

> *Did you know?*
>
> When Joe and number 22 try to taste the pizza, there is a broccoli pizza on the top row. This is a reference to the film *Inside Out*.

1053. How many times does number 22 slap Joe to demonstrate they do not have a sense of touch?
    a. Ten
    b. Eight
    c. Twelve
    d. Nine

1054. What is written on the sign when Joe talks to number 22 about becoming a librarian?
    a. Quiet
    b. Information
    c. Reference
    d. Library

> *Did you know?*
>
> The chemical formula on the board is the chemical composition of chocolate.

1055. What does number 22 suggest she try when Joe has to go to the great beyond?
    a. Ballet dancer
    b. Tap dancer
    c. Breakdancer
    d. Ice dancer

> *Did you know?*
>
> The wall of Hello badges from number 22 previous mentors include several Disney animators, including Joe Grant, Joe Ranft, and Jack Kirby.

> *Did you know?*
>
> Inside number 22's house, the Luxo Jr. ball can be seen next to the couch as the base of a table.

1056. Which team has number 22 been messing with for years in the zone?
    a. The White Sox
    b. The Knicks
    c. The Dodgers
    d. The Steelers

1057. What shape is the anchor on the ship for the Mystics without Borders?
    a. Peace symbol
    b. Heart
    c. Yin-yang
    d. Cloud

1058. What occupation does the lost soul have that the Mystics without Borders capture?
    a. Insurance agent
    b. Banker
    c. Hedge fund manager
    d. Schoolteacher

1059. What activity does the captain of the Mystics without Borders ship engage in that cause him to become a lost soul?
    a. Mario Bros.
    b. Scrabble
    c. Monopoly
    d. Tetris

1060. What is the name of the therapy cat at the hospital?
    a. Binx
    b. Mr. Mittens
    c. Salem
    d. Miss Whiskers

1061. After number 22 enters Joe's body, what does she call his fingers?
    a. Vienna sausages
    b. Meat sticks
    c. Toes
    d. Hand teeth

1062. How many times did number 22 fail the body test drive?

  a. Four hundred thirty-six times

  b. Four hundred sixty-three times

  c. Six hundred forty-three times

  d. Three hundred Forty-six times

Did you know?

Joe drags his body into room P742 at the hospital. This is a reference to P Sherman 42 Wallaby Way Sydney from the movie *Finding Nemo*. The letter P, seven letters in Sherman and the number 42.

Did you know?

When Joe steals the slice of pizza while in the cat's body, he sees a rat dragging a slice of pizza. This is a reference to the New York City subway rat meme that was widely popular in 2015.

1063. What color is the toothbrush number 22 uses in Joe's apartment?

  a. Red

  b. Yellow

  c. Blue

  d. Green

1064. What famous basketball player appears on the poster inside buddy's Barbershop?
    a. Wilt Chamberlain
    b. Kareem Abdul-Jabbar
    c. Kobe Bryant
    d. Walt Frazier

1065. What is the cost of a kids cut according to the price chart on the wall of Buddy's Barbershop?
    a. $45.00
    b. $10.00
    c. $16.00
    d. $20.00

1066. What type of business is to the left of Buddy's Barbershop?
    a. Nail salon
    b. Hair braiding
    c. Clothing store
    d. Shoe store

Did you know?

The travel agency poster that Joe walks by is an easter egg for the next Pixar film *Luca*. The poster reads Fly Luca Airways.

Did you know?

The subway car that Joe enters is car 2319. This is a reference to the Pixar movie *Monsters Inc.* Child Detection Agency code for a monster contaminated by a human object.

Did you know?

While riding the subway, there is an advertisement for the company Brang. This is a reference to the Pixar film *Inside Out*, the name of the company Riley's father works for.

1067. Joe's mother has a cross-stitch sampler on the wall with a sewing machine on it. Which of these is the quote on this sampler?
   a. Reap what you sew
   b. A stitch in time saves nine
   c. Sewing mends the soul
   d. A family stitched together by love seldom unravels

1068. What does Dorothea Williams call Joe when he shows up for the performance?
   a. Lunatic
   b. Crazy person
   c. Imbecile
   d. Nut case

1069. As Dorothea tells the story of the fish, what is the fish looking for?
   a. Nemo
   b. The EAC
   c. The ocean
   d. Her family

1070. Which key on the piano does Joe hit first when he returns home after the performance?
   a. A
   b. C
   c. D
   d. G

1071. Which of these is *not* one of the items Joe places atop his piano as he plays?
    a. Cat collar
    b. Pizza crust
    c. Leaf
    d. Lollipop stick

1072. What has become of number 22 after Joe enters the zone?
    a. She is a lost soul
    b. She is a mentor
    c. She entered the afterlife
    d. She is working for the Mystics without Borders

1073. What award did Terry ask for when he brought the count right?
    a. Medal
    b. Plaque
    c. Award
    d. Crown

1074. What does number 22 throw at Joe to stop him from following her?
    a. A lollipop
    b. Terry
    c. Rocks
    d. Souls

1075. What object does Joe give number 22 to stop the negative voices from attacking her?
    a. A spool of thread
    b. A lollipop
    c. A leaf
    d. A pizza crust

Did you know?

At the end of the credits, you will see Created & produced at Pixar Animation Studios "and in homes at least six feet away from each other through the bay area."

Conclusion

I hope you have enjoyed seeing your favorite films in a new way. My love for Disney/Pixar motivated me to write this book, and I have loved every moment of creating this book.

With each new movie, we will find creative innovation to bring the audience memorable favorites.

Answer Key

Toy Story

1. C – Saloon
2. D – Fifty Bzillion
3. C – Green
4. A – Rex
5. B – Piggy Bank
6. D – Reach for the sky
7. C – Built-in force field
8. A – The crib
9. C – Jump rope
10. A – Score
11. B – Home Sweet Home
12. C – Rattles
13. A – Princess Drool
14. C – Little Tikes
15. D – Picasso
16. B – Etch a Sketch
17. C – Five
18. A – Tinker toy box

19.   B – Thirty-five
20.   D – Tuesday
21.   D – Since kindergarten
22.   A – Recon Plan Charlie
23.   A – Barbeque
24.   C – Metal detector
25.   C – Forest Fantasy
26.   B – Cowboy costume
27.   A – Mother bird
28.   D – Power Cell
29.   B – Time for games
30.   D – Twelve
31.   C – Universe protection unit
32.   D – Turbo boosters
33.   A – Rex
34.   D – A Swiss Army Knife
35.   C – His wingspan
36.   B – Hamm
37.   C – Slinky Dog
38.   A – Coat hanger
39.   D – Tinkertoys
40.   C – Squeaky shark
41.   B – Scotch tape
42.   C – Summer camp
43.   D – Combat Carl
44.   A – Scud
45.   C – Virtual Realty
46.   B – Don't count on it
47.   A – Desk lamp
48.   D – Gallows

49. C – A bug
50. D – Pizza Planet truck
51. B – Yo
52. A – Super Nova Burger
53. C – 6,378, 531
54. B – Kabookey
55. D – The claw
56. C – Zealots
57. A – Alien
58. C – Hannah
59. B – 7:47
60. D – A hand
61. D – Cannibals
62. B – Whiskers
63. C – Bowl of milk
64. D – There's no place like home
65. C – Not a Flying Toy
66. A – Bowling
67. D – Mrs. Nesbit
68. A – Battleship
69. B – Eat them
70. D – Rex
71. A – Domino's
72. D – Dartboard
73. A – Match
74. D – Hakuna Matata
75. B – Mr. Potato Head
76. C – Her sheep
77. B – A Puppy

A Bug's Life

78.   A – Aphid
79.   D – Daisy
80.   A – Waterdrop
81.   B – The writer's children
82.   D – Flik's invention
83.   B – To get him out of the way
84.   C – A Dandelion
85.   B – Fly
86.   A – A Chinese coin
87.   D – Warriors
88.   D – Kids ripped my wings off
89.   B – Bottle caps
90.   A – O+
91.   B – Walking Stick
92.   C – A talent scout
93.   D – Snail shells
94.   B – *Picnic*
95.   C – Birds
96.   A – Ladybug

Toy Story II

97.   D – Zurg Vision
98.   B – A battery
99.   C – Jacks
100. B – Swallowed
101. A – Shmoes
102. A – Lawn gnome

103. D – Sweet potato
104. B – Chicken
105. C – Fourteen
106. B – Lincoln Logs
107. D – Thirteen and a half seconds
108. A – Toy arms
109. C – Stretch Armstrong
110. B – Wheezy
111. B – Peppermill
112. C – His watch
113. A – No early birds
114. D – LZTYBRN
115. C – Children
116. A – Clue
117. D – Abraham Lincoln
118. B – My ax is my best friend
119. A – Cowboy Crunchies
120. B – Fat
121. D – 12:00
122. A – The Grand Canyon
123. B – Sputnik
124. D – Orphans
125. B – Twenty-one
126. C – Licks his fingers
127. A – Cookie jar
128. D – Over six dollars
129. C – Road cones
130. B – Voice boxes
131. D – 6404.5
132. A – Steak

133. B – Wipe Out
134. A – Sixteen cars
135. B – Don't Eat the Jalapenos
136. D – Blue
137. A – Emily
138. C – Games
139. A – $12.99
140. B – Godzilla
141. D – Be the toy that comes with the meal
142. B – The box step
143. B – Rex
144. A – Torturing him
145. B – Feet
146. C – 546
147. D – Slinky Dog
148. B – A roll of packing tape
149. C – His pickaxe
150. A – Dime store
151. C – Beef Jerky
152. A – Ion blaster
153. A – Mr. Potato Head
154. D – Mr. Potato Head's hat
155. C – Wand of power
156. A – Heathrow Airport
157. C – Footprints
158. B – Mr. Shark

Monsters Inc.

159. D – 9:04
160. D – Soccer
161. B – Phlegm
162. A – Five
163. C – 8,400 SUV
164. A – Air Horn
165. D – Broom
166. B – One hundred twenty
167. C – Betty
168. D – Sulley's mom
169. A – Monstropolis Horn
170. C – Bilge berries
171. B – Eleven
172. C – Fur replacement
173. D – 13098
174. A – Thirteen
175. D – Sixteen
176. B – 99,351
177. C – One month
178. A – Fifty-eight
179. C – Shredder
180. B – Sock
181. B – Forty-seven
182. D – 374
183. C – Monster truck rally
184. A – Rotting Food
185. D – Teal
186. C – Flush them

187. A – Kitty
188. A – Sushi
189. C – Colander
190. B – Little Mikey
191. D – Cereal
192. B – Dive it to the country
193. B – Randall
194. B – Cinder blocks
195. C – Ushers
196. D – The scare floor will be painted
197. C – Autograph
198. A – Stephanie
199. D – Mike Wazowski
200. D – Mike
201. C – Lunch
202. B – Scream intake valve
203. C – A ride in his car
204. A – The Himalayas
205. D – Abominable snowman
206. B – Lingonberry
207. B – Lemon
208. D – King Itchy
209. C – Yak's milk
210. D – Insane
211. A – Mexico
212. C – Flowers
213. C – 01196
214. A – Roz
215. D – Mary
216. B – Jessie

217. B – Three
218. C – Bandits
219. D – Business Shriek
220. B – Drawing

Finding Nemo

221. A – Over four hundred
222. B – Anemone
223. A – Is there a hook in my lip?
224. D – Lucky Fin
225. C – Fluid rushing
226. B – Sandy Plankton
227. C – Snail
228. A – The sponge bed
229. D – Shrimp
230. A – Supraesophageal ganglion
231. C – She inks
232. C – Short term memory loss
233. B – Bruce
234. D – Mines
235. A – A recovery meeting
236. B – Step five
237. C – Sink
238. D – Three weeks
239. C – He never knew his father
240. A – Bloody nose
241. B – Submarine compartment
242. D – Barbara
243. C – Bubbles

244. B – eBay
245. A – Diving helmet
246. D – Hedstrom file
247. C – Pelican
248. B – Niece
249. A – Shook the bag
250. D – Didn't brush
251. B – Sea monkey
252. C – Diving mask
253. C – Grumpy gills
254. D – Bubbles
255. B – Shark Bait
256. A – Pebble
257. B – Jellyfish
258. D – Three weeks
259. A – Jellyfish
260. D – His bubbles
261. A – Readers Digest
262. B – Thrills
263. C – Just waxed it
264. A – Playing hide and seek
265. C – Jelly Man
266. D – Bob
267. B – Treated sewage
268. D – Rats with wings
269. C – Prime Minister
270. A – Swirling vortex of terror
271. C – One hundred fifty
272. B – Whale
273. D – Scum angels

274. C – Krill
275. A – Root beer float
276. B – Aqua Scum
277. C – Receiving an award
278. A – 82 degrees
279. D – Curse you
280. D – Rock N Roll Girl
281. B – Gerald
282. C – Angel's Cove
283. A – *Twinkle Twinkle Little Star*
284. B – Piranha
285. A – In the car
286. C – Alligator
287. D – Mirror
288. B – Exchange student
289. A – Harpo
290. B – Plastic bags

The Incredibles

291. C – The maid
292. D – KR 54
293. C – San Pablo Ave
294. B – Villaville
295. A – Shellmound Ave.
296. D – Squeaker
297. D – Brody
298. C – His flight pattern
299. B – Sansweet
300. A – WS2475

301. C – Pencil cup
302. D – Bernie
303. A – Robert
304. D – Tony
305. B – 440
306. B – Dissected a frog
307. C – Salmon
308. A – May 16, 1962
309. C – Honey
310. D – Robbery
311. D – *The Incredibles theme*
312. B – Rubble
313. C – Pigheadedness
314. A – The stockholders
315. B – Four
316. C – Omnidroid
317. D – Tilly
318. B – Bird camera
319. D – Fruit
320. A – A train
321. C – Thirty-six
322. D – The electric fence
323. B – Hobo suit
324. C – Sucked into a vortex
325. A – Shrimp cocktail
326. C – Pear
327. D – Egyptian cotton
328. B – Coconut
329. B – Moai
330. A – Evil plot

331. C – 8 hours 10 minutes
332. A – Mozart
333. D – The reflection in the water
334. C – Toothpick
335. A – Their identity
336. B – Doubt
337. B – Mirage
338. A – Bugs
339. C – His wife
340. D – Say please
341. D – Hai Karate
342. A – Her evening
343. C – The financial district
344. B – Record company
345. C – Sewer cover
346. A – Sneeze
347. D – Syndrome
348. B – Invisibility
349. A – Spartans
350. A – Popcorn
351. C – The underminer

Cars

352. D – Motion doctor
353. B – Nelson
354. C – Redneck Hill
355. B – Adult drip pans
356. D – 195
357. A – Sizzle

358. C – One lug nut
359. D – Head and Tail Lights
360. C – Spark plugs
361. C – Thirty-six weeks
362. D – Free bird
363. B – East Honkers
364. A – Top Down
365. B – Recycled batteries
366. A – 1909
367. C – Chachkies
368. B – Arnold Schwarzenegger
369. D – Sleeping Beauty
370. C – Take a blow torch to him
371. D – Tahiti
372. A – The way of justice is paved with truth
373. B – Thirty-two thousand dollars
374. D – Taillights
375. B – Lincoln continental breakfast
376. C – Nice Butte
377. D – Beemer
378. A – Freak juice
379. B – Pinstripe tattoo
380. D – Harvester
381. C – Stickers
382. A – *The National Anthem*
383. C – 1955
384. B – Ramone
385. C – VW Beetles
386. D – Smashing mailboxes
387. C – Fire engine

388. A – Crash
389. B – Fettuccini Alfredo
390. D – Guaranteed no tailgaters
391. C – Backfire
392. A – Scottsdale
393. C – Doc Hudson
394. A – Fifty
395. B – Tornado in a trailer park
396. C – Twenty-seven
397. A – Toy Car Story

Ratatouille

398. C – Five months
399. D – French Fare
400. B – The Grim Eater
401. C – Poison checker
402. A – Bottlecap
403. B – Music
404. D – TV Antenna
405. D – Fan
406. A – Umbrella stand
407. A – Spatula
408. C – Putting on lipstick
409. C – Renata
410. B – Peppermill
411. A – Colander
412. D – Potatoes
413. B – Twelve
414. D – Oven mitt

415. C – 7:08
416. D – Caviar
417. A – Two years
418. D – Whisk
419. C – Meat cleaver
420. B – Twelve
421. C – Stole the prime minister of France ball-point pen
422. A – Licorice
423. D – Some sort of wrapper
424. C – Matchsticks
425. B – Snobbery
426. C – Toothpaste cap
427. D – Baguettes
428. A – Pepper spray
429. C – Eggrolls
430. B – Chef Boyardee
431. A – Hamburgers
432. D – No smoking
433. C – A perfect day for a perfect Souffle
434. D – Bordeaux
435. B – Three months
436. A – Asparagus
437. C – His heart roasted on a spit
438. B – Gargoyle
439. D – Grill
440. C – Roller skates
441. A – A bicycle
442. C – Soccer ball
443. B – 114030
444. D – Spoon

WALL-E

445. D – *Hello Dolly*
446. B – Global CEO
447. C – Five years
448. D – Toaster
449. C – Evacuation sale
450. A – Pinwheel
451. D – Christmas ornaments
452. A – Classified
453. B – *Don't Worry, Be Happy*
454. D – Hand mixer
455. A – Rubik's Cube
456. D – Lighter
457. A – Crowbar
458. D – An old tire
459. B – Pong
460. C – Hit virtual golf balls
461. B – 72 degrees
462. A – John
463. D – Blue
464. A – A pool
465. B – Captain Fee
466. D – *The Blue Danube*
467. B – Cupcake in a cup
468. C – Operation recolonization
469. B – Get cleaned
470. A – Rogue
471. D – Welding
472. D – The garbage chute

473. B – 2110
474. A – Massage robot
475. B – Holding EVE's hand

UP

476. C – Movietown
477. D – Dirigible
478. B – An old house
479. C – 43,976
480. A – Bottlecap
481. D – Stick
482. B – A library book
483. C – Camera
484. B – Pink
485. A – Blimps
486. A – House flood
487. D – Bran
488. B – Shady Oaks
489. C – Sushi
490. B – Prune juice
491. D – Fifty-four
492. A – Azaleas
493. C – Blue
494. B – Airplane
495. B – Coffee grinder
496. C – Cumulonimbus
497. A – His dad
498. D – A billion
499. C – Garden hose

500. A – Parade balloon
501. D – Three days
502. B – Carl's hearing aid
503. A – Tigers
504. B – Kevin
505. D – Pink
506. A – Rocks
507. B – Hi there
508. D – Bengay
509. B – Doberman pinscher
510. C – Traveling flea circus
511. A – Frog
512. D – Small mailman
513. C – Stay
514. B – Paris
515. D – Roosevelt
516. A – Gin rummy
517. B – Cherries jubilee
518. A – His badges
519. B – Platypus
520. D – Leaf blower
521. A – Refrigerator
522. C – He loves him
523. A – Dog bones
524. B – Gray leader
525. D – His cane
526. B – He yells squirrel
527. B – Extreme mountaineering lore
528. A – Camping museum
529. B – Water glasses
530. C – Star Wars

Toy Story 3

531. D – Nunchuks
532. B – Troll dolls
533. C – Cattle skull
534. A – Death by monkeys
535. C – Slinky's butt
536. A – Rex
537. A – Shark
538. D – Super encyclopedia
539. C – Their accessories
540. A – Trashbag
541. C – Humble Beginnings
542. B – Tween
543. D – Hamm
544. D – Mechanical monkey
545. B – Jack in the box
546. A – *Dream Weaver*
547. C – GI Joe
548. A – Mr. Tony
549. D – Hopscotch
550. B – Sunflowers
551. C – Kite
552. D – *A Bug's Life*
553. A – Jessie
554. C – Egg carton
555. B – Hearts
556. C – Jelly beans
557. D – Monopoly® money
558. A – Coyote

559. D – Switch him to demo mode
560. B – Domino's
561. C – Mrs. Potato Head's lost eye
562. A – Her scarf
563. C – Sandbox
564. B – Potsie
565. B – Chuckles
566. D – Hamm
567. C – Tape
568. A – Tortilla
569. D – Rex
570. C – Paddleball
571. A – Silver space suit
572. A – Spanish
573. C – Dandelion
574. B – Toy telephone
575. D – Hearts
576. B – Television
577. B – Fan
578. B – The aliens
579. C – Loosen his stitching
580. D – Takes off his nose

Cars 2

581. C – Pear
582. A – Prop
583. D – Weapons designer
584. D – Pudding
585. C – Thirteen

586. B – The Incredimobiles
587. C – His new dent
588. A – Rearview Mirror
589. D – 324
590. B – Vacuum
591. B – Tires
592. D – Radiator
593. C – Wasabi
594. D – Gremlin
595. A – Electromagnetic Pulse
596. C – John Drippan
597. C – Miguel Camino
598. A – A58667A372159
599. D – Proper detailing
600. B – Car hood
601. B – Fire extinguisher
602. C – Nut
603. D – Imerawheel Hotel
604. B – Dead
605. A – Reliant Regal
606. B – New car smell
607. A – Dracula
608. D – His dents
609. C – Designing Iphone™ apps
610. B – Carla Veloso
611. C – Lemons
612. A – His clutch assembly broke
613. D – Brazil
614. A – Lunatic
615. C – Royal Radiators

616. C – Air filter
617. B – Calahan's
618. D – Ye Left Turn Inn
619. A – Red the firetruck
620. B – Range Rovers
621. C – Have a nice day
622. D – Luigi
623. C – Sarge

Brave

624. D – Scotland
625. B – Falcons
626. C – Merida's birthday
627. B – Will O' the wisps
628. A – Your fate
629. D – Spears
630. A – Leg
631. C – Harold
632. C – Apple
633. B – Her kingdom
634. C – Lyre
635. D – Chortle
636. A – Their haggis
637. A – Her bedpost
638. D – Muttering
639. D – Angus
640. A – Cut off half of his mustache
641. B – MacDonald
642. C – A log

643. D – Ten thousand
644. B – Troll
645. A – Bites him
646. D – Grabs them by the ears
647. D – Bear
648. C – Her bow
649. B – Fourteen
650. D – Half
651. A – The broom sweeps by itself
652. B – Everything
653. D – A Prince
654. C – A ring
655. A – A tart
656. B – A fortnight
657. A – Blueberries
658. A – Gamey
659. B – He smells it
660. D – Deer
661. C – Her desserts
662. C – Frog
663. D – Their kilts
664. B – Vial 3
665. A – Spring
666. C – The second sunrise
667. B – Lightning
668. D – Nightshade berries
669. B – Worms
670. C – A leaf
671. A – The elders
672. D – Through a well

673. C – Fire poker
674. B – Her brothers
675. A – Frying pan
676. B – Her mother
677. C – Merida's brothers

Monster's University

678. B – Frighton Elementary
679. A – No disappearing
680. D – A nickel
681. D – Football helmet
682. C – Ace my classes
683. B – First-semester bonfire
684. A – January 25
685. C – 319
686. D – Pink flamingos
687. A – 9:15
688. D – Scariness
689. B – Archie
690. B – Howl street
691. C – 102
692. A – BUFFMaster
693. C – A book
694. D – Scream can design
695. D – Textiles
696. B – New age philosophy
697. C – Couch cushions
698. A – Mom
699. B – Jaws Omega Roar

700. C – Stinging glow urchins
701. D – His everything
702. B – Use of illegal protective gel
703. D – Close up magic
704. A – Squishy
705. C – Squishy
706. D – Gunderson
707. B – Art
708. C – Gum
709. A – Hearts
710. C – Worthington
711. D – Sherry
712. B – "You look funny."
713. B – Camp Teamwork
714. A – A closet
715. C – A doll
716. A – 04114
717. D – Surprise her
718. C – The abominable snowman
719. A – Meet your new janitorial team

Inside Out

720. B – Thirty-three seconds
721. B – Broccoli
722. A – No dessert
723. C – Core memories
724. D – Monkey
725. D – They did not die
726. A – National Movers

727. C – Dollhouse
728. B – Rabies
729. C – Butterfly
730. A – Thursday
731. D – A mop
732. B – Sadness touches them
733. A – Reading mind manuals
734. A – A bear
735. C – Thirty-seven
736. D – Joy
737. B – Caramel Corn Curls
738. C – Accordion
739. B – Volcanic eruption
740. D – Seven
741. A – History
742. C – Long term memory
743. D – Greens
744. C – Sadness
745. C – Watching hockey
746. D – Put his foot down
747. B – Memory dump
748. A – Sadness
749. B – Vacuum them
750. A – Tripledent gum
751. C – Bing Bong
752. B – Wagon
753. D – Hippopotamus
754. C – Imagination land
755. D – DANGER
756. A – Apple juice

757. B – Loneliness
758. D – French fries
759. B – House of cards
760. C – Fear
761. D – Teddy bear
762. A – Fear
763. B – Attack of the fluffy puppies
764. D – Dog
765. C – Subconscious
766. A – Neighbors big dog
767. C – Balloons
768. B – Tell him there is a birthday party
769. A – Mental blocks
770. B – Honesty island
771. C – Take her to the moon for me, ok?
772. B – Perfect boyfriend
773. A – A chair
774. C – Sadness
775. D – Boy band island
776. B – The Bahamas
777. B – Fear

The Good Dinosaur

778. A – Use their tails
779. B – Mouth
780. D – Tammy
781. D – Chicken
782. B – Mud
783. C – Cluckers

784. A – Firefly
785. C – Catch the critter that eats their food
786. B – Wooden log
787. A – Find the river
788. A – Tripped over a rock
789. C – The first snow
790. D – Leaves
791. C – The human digs him out
792. B – A lizard
793. B – A snake
794. D – Mosquitos
795. C – Annihilator
796. D – Debbie
797. B – Spot
798. C – Twigs
799. A – T rex
800. A – Velociraptors
801. D – A bug
802. B – He does not have footprints
803. D – Spot finds his family

Finding Dory

804. B – Sand
805. A – Undertow
806. B – Bottles
807. D – Pinata
808. B – Stingray migration
809. A – Instinct
810. C – Jewel

811. A – Crush
812. D – Charlie
813. B – They will worship him
814. D – Six-pack rings
815. C – 3181
816. A – Cleveland
817. B – Coffee
818. A – Laying on the rock
819. A – Gerald
820. D – A planter
821. C – Shells
822. B – Whale shark
823. D – The pipes
824. A – Becky
825. A – Baby stroller
826. C – Three
827. B – Hands
828. D – He inks
829. C – Trying to get a purple shell for her mom
830. B – Two lefts and a right
831. B – Echolocation
832. A – Forgetting
833. C – Cupcake
834. D – Her eyes
835. C – Sea otters
836. B – Becky
837. C – Seagulls
838. A – *What a Wonderful World*
839. C – Substitute teacher

Cars 3

840. D – Doc Hudson
841. B – 196
842. C – Natalie
843. A – Wind resistance
844. D – Dinoco
845. B – The Daily Exhaust
846. C – The Sistine Chapel
847. A – Trunk
848. A – Los Angeles Motor Speedway
849. B – Trainer
850. D – Four
851. C – Drinking fountain
852. B – Ambulance
853. D – A fossil
854. A – Hamilton
855. C – Crab
856. A – No cursing
857. B – Taxicab
858. A – License plates
859. D – Doyle
860. C – Hay bails
861. B – Forty-three
862. D – 51
863. B – Lizzie
864. B – Ice cream truck

Coco

865. A – Día De Los Muertos
866. C – Blue
867. D – Making pottery
868. C – Julio
869. B – Five
870. D – 1921
871. A – Dante
872. C – Her sandal
873. A – Papa Julio
874. C – Mole
875. D – Eating
876. A – The crypt of Ernesto De La Cruz
877. D – Someone walks through him
878. B – The marigold bridge
879. C – Spirit creatures
880. A – Bienvenidos
881. D – Churros
882. B – He sinks into the petals
883. C – His nose
884. B – Devil box
885. A – Pan dulce
886. D – Sunrise
887. C – Her Alebrije
888. C – Shoe polish
889. B – Chorizo
890. A – They fade
891. C – Accordions
892. A – Sousaphone

893. C – Porcupine
894. B – He sings
895. C – Polo
896. D – Chihuahua
897. C – Poison his drink
898. A – Success
899. A – To see his daughter
900. C – Imelda
901. B – Her shoe
902. D – Ernesto's crypt
903. C – He sings to her
904. A – His letters

The Incredibles 2

905. D – File 82-712
906. B – She takes her mask off
907. D – Spartans
908. C – Frozone
909. C – City Hall
910. D – Nothing
911. A – Safari Court
912. B – Godzilla
913. C – Chief executive officer
914. A – Dynaguy
915. D – Designer
916. B – Ignorance
917. B – Basketball
918. D – Grapes
919. A – Blue

920. D – She had a mohawk
921. B – Sugar Bombs
922. D – Doozles dozing
923. D – Tribune
924. B – His high tops
925. A – 1954
926. A – Seal
927. B – Racoon
928. A – Transfiguration
929. A – 2:17
930. C – On his locker
931. B – KQRY
932. D – Ninety-two
933. D – Slice of cake
934. B – Philodendrons
935. C – Johnny Quest
936. B – Mozart
937. D – Blackberry lavender
938. A – Free
939. D – Pizza delivery guy
940. C – A cookie
941. A – Kisses him
942. C – She knocks over a plant
943. B – Jack Jack
944. A – Krushaur
945. D – Happily ever after
946. C – *Dementia 113*

Toy Story 4

947. A – RC car
948. B – McGee
949. C – Operation pull toy
950. D – Baker
951. B – Jessie
952. A – Roger
953. C – Hat shop owner
954. D – Miss Wendy
955. C – Anton
956. B – Apple
957. D – Trash
958. A – Rainbow
959. C – Dipping sauce containers
960. B – Pudding
961. A – 5.32 miles
962. A – Vincent
963. D – Harmony
964. C – Typewriter
965. D – A spoon
966. C – Five
967. A – Frisbee
968. D – Safety pin
969. A – Pinata
970. A – Astro boy
971. D – Their tongues
972. B – Carousel
973. C – A nail
974. D – Dragon

975. A – Croquet mallet
976. D – Hide and go seek
977. B – Pinball machine
978. C – Her accessory
979. D – Doug
980. B – Ten
981. A – Rejean
982. B – 8mm film
983. C – Popcorn
984. D – Time for donuts
985. A – What's new pussy cat?
986. C – Giggles McDimple
987. B – Pencil
988. D – His voice box
989. A – Buzz Lightyear
990. C – Low-fat lard
991. D – Wooden blocks
992. B – A ventriloquist doll
993. C – Trixie
994. A – Baseball
995. B – Lock the car doors
996. D – His badge

Onward

997. C – Woodless
998. A – Crystal
999. A – Unicorns
1000. B – Chess club meeting
1001. D – Blazey